PEOPLE POWER

Reading People For Results

By
Elizabeth I. Kearney, Ph.D.
Michale J. Bandley, Ph.D.

Sterling Press

PREFACE

EFFECTIVE COMMUNICATION IS LITERALLY PEOPLE POWER, and there is no facet of our lives that does not involve the need for effective communication.

- It dictates the harmony of our relationships
- It relates to our success as motivators and managers
- It affects the teamwork in any organization
- It "makes or breaks" a sale
- It is the cause of most conflicts
- It is the source of all success.

Once we recognize this, and relize that we can serve others better, enjoy our work and lives more, and ensure our own success by learning the basic techniques of READING PEOPLE, then we have but one realistic course of action—get the information we need and make the tools work for us.

This book is designed to give you the information, introduce you to the tools (one of the most useful is the problem solving wheel which appears in the appendix and is explained in one of the chapters), and then the rest is up to you.

DEDICATION

We want to thank those whose support and effort made this book possible. Their help and support were essential and most appreciated. We also could not have met our deadline if Analee Perica had not been willing to work long hours to make certain that the first draft was the last.

This book was a cooperative effort. It provides the help needed to build those vital communication bridges throught the power of reading, understanding, and adjusting to others.

TABLE OF CONTENTS

CHAPTER	PAGE
PREFACE	i
DEDICATION	ii
1: MAKING IT WORK	1
2: YOU—THE IMPORTANT INGREDIENT	9
3: RECOGNIZING OTHERS	19
4: VALUES: THE REAL POWER BASE	29
5: THE ART OF COMPATIBILITY	47
6: SELLING IDEAS TO OTHERS	77
7: STRESS: THE ROADBLOCK TO SUCCESS	93
8: HARNESS YOUR CREATIVE POWER	111
9: MANAGING: AN ART AND A SCIENCE	129
10: THE HIRING EDGE	147
11: TEAMS: THE WAY TO GO	161
12: THE CHANGING WORKPLACE	181
APPENDIX:	197
SUMMARY OF KEY POINTS	198
SELF CHECK	200
PEOPLE CHECK	202
THE SOLUTION IS IN YOUR HANDS	206
AN INVITATION FROM THE AUTHORS	209
ORDER FORM	211

PREVIEW POINT

People are the key ingredient in all human activity, yet all too often successful interaction is left to chance. This book provides you with the tools and techniques to take chance out of your communication and puts knowledge in.

1

MAKING IT WORK
FOR YOU

Alexander Pope once said, "The proper study of mankind is man," and yet most people tend to "judge" others by themselves. We accept the idea that each person should be viewed as an individual, but we then assume that all are like us. WRONG!! Research and practical experience prove this false.

WHY READ PEOPLE?

People are the key ingredient in all human activities, yet all too often successful interaction is left to chance. Then, who should learn how to read people? EVERY-ONE!

One of the biggest problems in society today is poor communication within families, and the family structure is in trouble, as a consequence. Each child needs to be treated as an individual and consideration should be given to his or her needs and abilities. Since this is the case, it is imperative that parents learn to recognize and understand the behavioral styles and differences of their children and learn how to meet their individual and identified needs.

Marital difficulties arise most frequently because of a lack of communication, and statistics show that 50% of all marriages end in divorce. NO ONE MARRIES PLANNING TO DIVORCE LATER, SO WHAT GOES WRONG? It is crucial that anyone entering into such a relationship be able to understand the other person and read and respond appropriately to the clues given—both verbal and—especially—non-verbal.

Holidays and the related family gatherings are often one of the major sources of periodic stress. Many people go into depressions at such times, and illnesses increase. WHY? The conflicts and tensions generated by misunderstandings and "hurt" feelings are the culprits. Yet, this tension and stress could be avoided. Since by understanding people, it is possible to know when to respond, how to respond, and when not to respond.

One's circle of friends generally encompasses a wide variety of people. Although some of us have only a few

REALLY close friends, we do have numerous acquaintances. In order to understand our close friends, we need to recognize their needs and know when to back off, when to help, when to listen, and how to encourage them.

Our daily lives bring us into contact with many people with whom we interact and whom we like, but we may not develop a deep friendship with them for a wide variety of reasons. Nevertheless, in order to have a good working relationship or good interaction, we need to understand them and their behavioral patterns. Thus, we can communicate effectively with good results.

Each day brings the average person into contact with numerous people from the business world—

clerks, doctors, contractors, etc., yet conflict may arise because each person could have a different point of view about the service or materials delivered. Because this occurs, it is necessary to understand the signals which people give and be able to adjust your own approach or behavior to maximize results. Productivity and profit are the key ingredients in the success of any company, but low morale and poor interaction among the personnel can sabotage a company's growth. The different personalities found within any company need to be considered since management must be able to understand each behavioral style in order to get the results needed and insure both productivity and profit.

Success on the job is a motivator in and of itself, yet many times it is determined by the interaction within the division or company. A lack of cooperation among the staff can affect not only the company's productivity and profit, but also the morale of the people who work there. It is, therefore, necessary for people to be aware of and able to recognize the differences among people.

Many of us need to equate our personal worth to the success of our undertakings, and yet we fail to realize that in many instances our success is tied closely to our ability to relate to and interact with others. Since this is the case, close attention needs to be paid to our communications styles, and this is true for all professions.

For example, the success of all **doctors** is in direct proportion to their ability to relate to their patients and colleagues.

Lawyers, on the other hand, need to work harmoniously with their colleagues and clients, but also be able to interact effectively with and adjust to the behavioral styles of the jurors in order to win their cases or secure the best possible settlements or judgment.

Engineering is a highly technical profession, and those in it tend to have a unique style which makes it possible for them to deal in abstractions with success. Yet, this very talent also makes it difficult for some of them to communicate effectively with others or interact with other types of individuals.

Communication is, of course, the key to the success of any educational program, and it is important for those in this field to be able to relate to and communicate with not only the students, but also their colleagues, administrators, and the students' parents. Without this ability, educators may not be able to make a positive difference in a child's education and future life.

No **sale** can take place until a sound communication bridge has been built, so it is crucial for all of those in **sales** to understand and be able to adjust the approach used to the behavioral styles and needs of the clients.

In many ways, we are all in sales—we sell ideas, concepts, products, or services—every time we come in contact with others. So, there is seldom a day that passes that would not require us to "read people" if we are to reach our goals and succeed in our undertakings.

Successful communication builds and develops trust, and trust allows successful interaction. By "reading" people properly, your ability to communicate is enhanced. Remember communication is both transmitting and receiving.

KEY POINT #1

YOU ARE RESPONSIBLE
FOR THE WAY
YOU RESPOND TO PEOPLE.

PREVIEW POINTS

You are a visible reflection of your values, your thinking strengths and weaknesses, and influential experiences in you life. Others see the "face" you want them to see plus the "faces" you may well hide from them and yourself most of the time. The most successful among us get in touch with themselves, learn to understand their motivators, and seek to "read," understand, and accept others.

2

YOU—THE IMPORTANT
INGREDIENT

T he "you" the world knows is really a composite of many different components, and your behavior is the visible reflection of the interaction of all of the components.

Did you know that each of your actions is pre-shaped? Well it is! Your values determine what you do, and your brain dominance patterns determine how well you do it. Some of us insist that we be given every little detail, and other say, "Oh, for heaven's sake skip all that—just get to the bottom line." Then, there are those who are really driven to obtain money or what it can buy while their opposites just want enough to keep them alive and healthy. These two values, research and affluence, are coupled with four more—beauty, control, structure, and interaction, and, again, you are motivated to act by the level of need in each.

YOU—THE IMPORTANT INGREDIENT.

Just listen to those around you, and you will begin to be able to identify those values they stress and those upon which they place little value. For example, we all know a person who can't move into an office or a home until it looks "perfect," but someone else may well work happily in a basement cubbyhole and not even notice the surroundings. And, of course, we have all been to the meeting where one person—not the one who was chairing it—took control of the meeting when the one in charge seemed unable to do so. Those two were at opposite ends of the control value scale. Does it make a difference to them? To you? You bet it does!

Let's look at another example. Have you tried to live or work with those who seem to "destroy" structure and who bring chaos into every situation? It may not have bothered you, if you had a similar pattern, but if you are one who must have a place for everything and everything in its place, you probably had trouble coping. The same would be true of those who had differing interactive levels. The person who seemed to be born with a "telephone cord" instead of an umbilical cord could be very upsetting to someone who prefers as few human contacts as possible or who sees excessive interaction as a waste of time or money. Each of us is quite a unique combination of these six values (research, beauty, affluence, interaction, control, and structure), and it is this variation which shapes many aspects of our behavior. The individual combinations are shaped by many variables, and the end result is an invisible, but powerful, force in each person's life.

Although we are directed by those values, it is our intellect that makes it possible for our actions to be performed at a given level of attainment and in a given way. Some years ago, a Dr. Sperry at California Institute of Technology in Pasadena, California, set up experiments which resulted in a new awareness of the working of the human mind. He found that the brain performed different—but related—functions in the left and right hemispheres. Later research showed that this division could be taken even further, and that various functions are localized in the brain's quadrants. For example, the upper left quadrant seems to control one's analytical and logical analysis while the lower left appears to be "in charge" of organizational and structural thinking. The right hemisphere controls interaction and visualization.

To many this sounds very esoteric, but it has a very practical impact. What we do and how well we do it are governed by these quadrants. For example, the boss who hates details would be wise to hire an associate who loves them, and the spouse who can't balance the checkbook will need a counterpart who checks every detail. In other words, what happens in one of those quadrants, has a very direct and important impact upon what happens in our world.

Several years ago we were called into a company concerned enough about one employee to take the steps needed to find out why a very competent person was literally "coming apart" and failing to perform in a consistently productive way. We used the assessment instruments we developed and use with many of our clients to assess drive, interaction, rule compliance, and pace levels; values patterns; and brain dominance.

What we learned came as a shock to us all. This highly successful systems design engineer, was succeeding in her field by sheer determination and desire. She was one who really was most comfortable interacting with people in a creative way to solve problems and produce alternative solutions, but she did not like detail work. We can do anything we want to do if we want to do it badly enough, but when it is not a basically natural process, we have to work harder at it, expend more energy, and may well suffer emotional or physical consequences as a result.

That was the case, and what they saw as lowered productivity and diminished morale were the consequences of a mounting tension and fatigue. We were lucky—and so were they—there were two systems design engineers, and the other was a mirror to her. We merely restructured the assignments and made them into the team they had always been called, but never really were.

When the values systems' motivational power is coupled with the intellect's potential, we get a personality which is reflected to the rest of the world through behaviors, and these behaviors—ours and those of others—make it essential that we take the time to learn more in order to take a power seat in the communication game.

Our behavioral styles have several faces—the PUBLIC face which is a combination of the *projected* style (that behavior that we want to have you see) and our *latent* style which appears when we are under stress/ pressure or in a state of complete relaxation. At those times, we tend to remove the mask we normally wear, the one T. S. Eliot referred to when he said, "We put on a face to meet the faces we meet," and let you see another side of us, a side that may shock us as well as you.

Those who are the most successful are those who have been able to understand and respond equally well to people in their myriad combinations. Each of us is a composite of our values and intellect which in turn creates our personalities which others see through our behaviors.

Our research has shown that there are six behavioral styles which combine into myriad behavioral patterns. Each of us behaves according to these styles and combinations, and there is, therefore, a degree of predictability to our actions. It is for this reason, that some of the world's most successful salespeople have said that they "read" their customers or clients and then know how to sell or close. If this is their key to success, shouldn't it be yours?

BEHAVIORAL CLUES

STYLES	JOB	DRESS	DESK	PACE	WANTS
LEADER	Authority	Corp.	Org. stacks	Fast	Results
PERSUADER	People rel.	Fash.	Messy	Fast	Results
PATIENT	Specialized	Classic	Neat	Unhur.	Process
CAREFUL	Precise	Matched	Organized	Consid.	Process
RESERVED	Idea based	*	Uncluttered	Consid.	Process
INDEPEN	Entrep.	**	Several	Fast	Results

* like either the PATIENT OR CAREFUL person, but dresses at a given time and forgets it.
**whatever he/she pleases according to what he/she wants.

The first step is to determine your own style. Although it is possible to learn drive, interaction, pace, rules compliance levels as well as confusion, tension, depression, and stress of both the latent and public profiles from one of our assessment tests, for now, let's just take a look at your public behaviors. After all, it is your public behavior that others see most often. SELF CHECK (in the appendix) will identify your own style and provide you with the base for utilizing the information shared in later chapters.

Productivity and profit are the cornerstones of business success, and an increasing number of businesses and corporations are realizing that the key to both is effective interaction/communication. It is for this reason that they are providing training in people skills both to managers and staff. Once people realize that adjustments are needed and that people's styles differ (notice the plural, we are often more than one style), the major barrier to effective communication is destroyed, and it is possible to communicate, motivate, and cooperate with far greater ease.

KEY POINT #2

OUR SUCCESS IS TIED CLOSELY TO OUR ABILITY TO RELATE TO AND INTERACT SUCCESSFULLY WITH OTHERS.

PREVIEW POINTS

RESULTS ARE THE NAME OF THE GAME, and effective interaction requires that you build a communication bridge . This means that you need to realize that "each man " in his time plays many parts," to recognize those parts (styles) , and to adjust to—and for—them.

3

"NO MAN IS AN ISLAND"

RECOGNIZING OTHERS

John Donne was not talking about communication nor interpersonal skills when he said, that "no man is an island," but his statement holds true nevertheless. No facet of human endeavor is possible without some degree of successful interaction and communication.

Most people do not consciously try to analyze others as they interact, but on a subconscious level many factors are considered. For example, we may well wonder if people are angry if they frown as we are talking to them, or decide that they are unsure when they tilt their heads. In other words, we do process and form opinions as we note gestures, eye movements, speech patterns, posture, accents, and dress.

Our own background shapes our reactions and responses to these signals which—in turn—were shaped by the other person's background, too. We need to be in a position to process this information in a meaningful and usable way, and it is the purpose of this book to help you do so.

When you read the behavioral clues accurately, you improve your personal relationships, management techniques, self-esteem, approach to team building, credibility, increase your productivity, and improve your morale.

It is not what you know, but what you DO with what you know that COUNTS. RESULTS ARE THE NAME OF THE GAME, and the clues we are about to share have to be put to use and the techniques practiced before they will help you. Don't just guess about what a person wants or doesn't want; likes or doesn't like; reacts to negatively or positively when you can KNOW by reading the other person. Just note five clues-dress, speech, manner, setting, body language, and career.

Does that sound impossible—well, it isn't!! Just use PEOPLE CHECK (see appendix) according to the directions, and you will find out that you can gain the communication edge easily and quickly. After you have used this instrument (which we have now used as the base of a computer software program that provides in-depth information plus specific tips for successful interaction), you will better understand the information appearing on the following pages.

Life would be less complicated if all people were alike, but it would also be far less interesting. Think of how boring it would be if the world were peopled by humanoids. The same differences that make people fascinating and interesting are those that make it difficult for individuals who aren't "people readers" to communicate.

You will need some specific information if this system is to work for you and here are the highlights that will give you a new awareness of people.

ARE YOU DEALING WITH A LEADER? Well, you need to listen more than you talk to that person, stress results, and be prepared to work hard. It will also be important for you to be very business-like, let that person have control, and never pressure. It would be wise to develop some alternatives to problems you want solved and let the LEADER decide which alternative should be used, but while you are doing that DO NOT, repeat DO NOT,dwell on details or get bogged down in data. Share the big picture and provide the back-up data if it is requested. Remember this person is results-oriented, moves fast, and hates to waste time, and details are often thought to be too time consuming. Don't be surprised if this person is very direct—even blunt—at times, and don't lose your cool or "cave in." Both would diminish you in the person's mind.

PERHAPS YOU ARE DEALING WITH A PERSUADER? If you are working with one, then you need to remember that PERSUADERS are people-oriented as well as friendly, outgoing, and very interested in others. They love to talk and talk and talk, and they may have a tendency to jump to conclusions or avoid details and routines. They are impulsive and enthusiastic, and they truly enjoy recognition and beautiful surroundings. Take time to relate to them and find common interests and mutual friends, be interested in them as people, but above all, BE WARM.

MAYBE THE PERSON IS PATIENT. In order to make certain that your relationships with PATIENT PEOPLE work, you will need to remember that they are relaxed and congenial, but they also dislike change unless they are one of the change agents or had time to adjust. In addition, they are often very traditional in their approach and support the status quo.

Because they are analytical and thorough, they are careful to weigh the pros and cons before they take action on a given issue. This tendency may make them appear indecisive when they are really just dissecting the data. You need to remember that PATIENT PEOPLE resist pressure, need their questions answered thoroughly and patiently, and react best when ideas are presented or "sold" on an incremental basis.

COULD THE PERSON BE CAREFUL? Those perfectionists in your world need to be assured of the safety of an undertaking, but when that assurance is given they are open to new ideas. Their organizational skills are coupled with a desire to be accurate, a need to be concise, and an urge to be careful and detailed. You need to remember that those ideas you present or those projects you propose need to be explained in terms of the safety of the investment—time or money—and the ROI (return on investment). In addition, don't try to do a "hard sell" since they tend to be very suspicious of salespeople in general, and pushy ones in particular. Be accurate, supportive, and dollar prudent.

THE PERSON MAY BE RESERVED. Logic plays a major role in the lives of RESERVED PEOPLE, and you need to realize that although they may not be gregarious or outgoing, they are excellent friends to those whom they admit to their inner circle. They are most comfortable with those who are straight forward, logical, and respectful of their time and privacy, so you need to remember that and also avoid small talk which they may well see as a waste of time. You don't need to sell RESERVED PEOPLE—it won't work anyway, but if the information you share leads sequentially and logically to a given course of action or conclusion, they will "sell" themselves. They make decisions only after careful analysis and consideration of all ideas, concepts, and details, so be certain to provide them and be businesslike and self-controlled even if they are blunt.

IS THE PERSON AN INDEPENDENT? Ambition coupled with an innovative approach are the basis for the entrepreneurial approach to business employed by most INDEPENDENTS. They are also likely to want direct answers, find rules confining, and be put off by those who insist on dwelling on details rather than the big picture. They enjoy doing things "their own way," and enjoy projects when they are told what needs to be done and are then left alone to get the results wanted. In fact, they are likely to believe that anything is possible—it may be that a new approach is needed. Because of this high level of self-confidence, they will tackle anything, even those projects for which there are no guidelines or precedents. At the same time, they may take stands, state their ideas pointedly, be blunt as they challenge you, and debate points just for the fun of it. If what you say interests them, they will probably "buy" into it, but only if you don't belabor the details.

Shakespeare was right when he said the "each man in his time plays many parts," and it is rare they anyone is just one of the above styles. It is far more likely that you will encounter combinations, and you must, therefore, "read" the combinations and realize that there are times when one style is dominant and other times when another style is.. Read the person in front of you now — not the person you KNEW yesterday nor the one you think you will encounter later. If you will do that one a consistent basis, you will assure your own success edge.

KEY POINT #3

IT IS NOT WHAT YOU KNOW BUT WHAT YOU DO WITH WHAT YOU KNOW THAT PROVIDES THE RESULTS AND DETERMINES THE WINNERS.

PREVIEW POINTS

Our values are the foundations upon which we build our lives and destiny, and it is by them that we are known.

4

VALUES:
THE REAL POWER BASE

T he world sees and judges us by our behaviors, but behind those behaviors are a number of variables. We do whatever we do because of our value system, and each of us does it at a given level of achievement and competency because we utilize the quadrants of our brain in accordance with our basic thinking patterns and strengths.

If we learn to identify and understand the six value motivators and recognize those things that are of the greatest worth and interest to us and others, we will be in a better position to relate and interact—the basis of true PEOPLE POWER.

VALUES: THE REAL POWER BASE

> - **R**   research or truth
> - **B**   beauty
> - **A**   affluence
> - **S**   structure
> - **I**   interaction
> - **C**   control

Our values are shaped by many things—our child-hood, our heros, our experiences, our religion or the belief system which we hold, and, although we do not consciously control it, we can shape it. Because we develop our values over a lifetime, they are not always logically aligned. In addition, there are times when the values themselves are in conflict. An individual may have a real need to adhere to rules and live by a philosophical structure, yet he may also need to conquer new worlds—worlds in which no rules exist or where it seems necessary to work or live without precedent. The resultant conflict may be great and even physically detrimental.

The person who places great stress on the value of effective interaction, may truly hurt when there is a need to criticize or discipline another.

In addition, situations arise which cause us to shift in order to survive at a level acceptable to us. For example, a woman who grew up in a protective home environment where all material needs were met for her and whose husband provided the same support might not display the same drive level in the area of affluence as she might later if death or divorce deprived her of those support systems. If she found a real need for money, she might well shift her level of drive (control) upward in order to perform the tasks needed to secure that money or security. Such a shift will alter her behaviors and be visible to us.

There has been no achievement in the history of mankind that has not been the direct result of an individual's or group's desire to reach certain goals or accomplish certain tasks. Wars are fought because a country wants more land or more power or because another group values its freedom and country enough to defend against the aggressors. Great art is the expression of artists who seek to create or recreate the beauty and meaning they see in their world, and power has been one of mankind's greatest motivators.

In order to achieve true PEOPLE POWER, we need to rid ourselves of certain misconceptions. Even though we know that others do not necessarily hold the same values as we do, we tend to act and interact as if they did—and conflicts or misunderstandings occur. These misunderstandings occur in marriage and in business, and although the consequences are quite different, the problem is the same—a lack of awareness and understanding. Each person strives to achieve his or her goals—whatever they are. And when we are interacting with others, there is a need to make certain that our goals either match their's or we understand and adjust for the differences. For example, money has long been a motivator—many times it is the most powerful of the six—yet a recent survey of some 500 people showed us that it motivates only until the level of need set by a given person is met. Once that level has been met, basic necessities for one person and a mansion for another, it is no longer the prime determinant. One CEO remembers when money was is a chief motivator, but he made enough money to satisfy his needs. Now money is not what is driving him to continue working—he wants to have a company which holds the most powerful position in the industry. He has met his monetary needs; now he wants power (control).

We may find that our world is filled with others just like us, but it is doubtful that you live in a world of clones. Therefore, we need to recognize and meet the needs of others—our family, our employees, our colleagues—and design and implement, or help them design and implement, effective approaches to meet those needs and satisfy those values. Once needs are met, they are no longer motivators, so it is necessary to recognize and meet those that have yet to be fulfilled.

Our values are influenced by many different variables, and it is not logical to assume that everyone is influenced by the same things. Even in our families we can see this. Two children can be brought up by the same parents, interact with the same people, attend the same school, go to the same church, and yet be markedly different in many ways. One may be almost compulsively neat and the other extremely sloppy; one thrifty and the other a spendthrift; and one studious and the other just gets by academically. The parents can't take all the credit or the discredit for such differences—there are too many factors—many of which we don't even recognize.

As you work with others, it will become more and more obvious that values are based upon both logic and emotion. When logic is the base, reasonable explanations or arguments can lead to change; when emotions are the base, pressure to change can result in hostility, anger, and even irrational reactions. Our values guide us, and our attitudes—whatever they may be—are a direct outgrowth of our value system. What ever we value will be viewed in a positive way, and anything that interferes with it, will be viewed negatively. For example, those who value their own independence, will resent it when others attempt to direct or pressure them.

When our attitudes match those exhibited by the society in which we live and the environment in which we work, they are considered positive one and may well lead to our success. However, when they do not match, it is likely that they will be deemed inappropriate, negative, or even detrimental by others.

Values can change, and when they do, they result in behavioral shifts, and it is those shifts that are seen by the world around us. Since most of us believe that our mirror reflects the world as it should be, we hold firmly to our values and attitudes and are suspicious of those who differ. Yet, situations change and the pressures created seem to domino. A recent divorcee told us that she had never been interested in money— earning or saving, but after her divorce, she realized that she had to make far more in order to maintain the lifestyle she preferred. Her focus shifted, and when she was retested, her values profile indicated that she now put a high value on affluence and control—the former to support her preferred way of life; the latter to provide the drive needed to control and shape her world to make it possible.

If we could visualize the pebble effect of "being," we would see that our view of ourself is shaped by our values which in turn are reflected in our attitudes. Our interests are the direct link to those attitudes, and the role/s we play (our behaviors) are the visual representations of all three. The same is true of the others in our world, and when this is taken into account, we can see why we relate best to the people most like us.

THAT IS NOT ENOUGH. We need to be able to adjust to the people and the demands of our world. In order to do this effectively, we must learn to identify our values and the values of those around us. The following sections will provide the guidelines to make this possible.

RESEARCH OR TRUTH
(Details and Process)

STRONGLY VALUED:
>Those who register high in this value are seeking "truth" and answers, and they want to know all of the details before they take any action. They also need to have information presented to them in a logical, sequential way, but even then, they may well question, critique, or even over-study project or undertakings. It is also likely that this person will enjoy working alone on ideas and concepts, be suspicious of those who are overly gregarious, and prefer that others not violate their privacy or ask too many questions.

LESS VALUED:

>Those who place little value on research or "truth" are inclined to reach their decisions rapidly with minimal data. They rely heavily on intuition and instinct, and emotion is often a guide. They are inclined to be more interested in the people involved and their reactions than in the facts or data that might be available.
>
>They may well express their "gut reaction" to given situations instead of their "considered opinion," and they need both interaction and psychic income.

BEAUTY
(Surroundings and Personal Adornment)

STRONGLY VALUED:

>Those who place a strong value on beauty are inclined to need and seek it in their world. They either produce the grace and harmony they need, or they turn to activities and settings that provide it. Remember, beauty "is [truly] in the eye of the beholder." Whatever their taste, it is still probable that they have definite ideas about design, color, detail, positioning of objects, and demand the right to deal with

them as they choose. Harmony is also important, and they are upset when anything upsets that harmony.

LESS VALUED:

The people who fit in here are far less concerned about form than they are the utilitarian aspects of any item. They need to know what it can do, how fast it will go, how long it will last, and what it will cost. In other words, articles are judged by a very practical yardstick. Durability, monetary value, and profit margin are far more important to these people than form, design, style, harmony, or beauty.

Those who place a high value on the beauty of their world often consider those who don't as declasé; and those who do not place such a value on beauty often see those who do as impractical.

AFFLUENCE
STRONGLY VALUED:

When one is motivated by affluence—money or what money can purchase—there is a tendency to consider the monetary worth of projects, products, or plans as a gauge for becoming involved.

Such people are practical, inclined to consider ideas, objects, and projects valuable in direct proportion to their utility, investment potential, or monetary value—present or future. They are often ambitious and interested in moving up the income ladder, and they take pride in their own success in a profit center. They also admire success.

They are not only acquisitive but also competitive, and they often dress in the latest cuts, styles, colors and fabrics. In fact, it is not unusual to find that they place value on well-known brands.

LESS VALUED:

Those who place a low value on affluence, tend to disregard material goods and find, instead, value in such intangibles as personal service, and relationships—both personal and spiritual. They often select careers that allow them to serve others—particularly the underdog and the disadvantaged.

They may not be too interested in business, for profit and productivity are of far less interest than people and process. If in business, they are often excellent in human resource management.

STRUCTURE
STONGLY VALUED:

> Those who place a high value on structure are often involved in their religion—even if it is not a formally recognized one, and they are likely to adhere to a strong code of ethics. They also seek approval from a higher source of good and strive to follow a firmly entrenched code of conduct.

> Right is right and wrong is wrong, and there are few grey areas. As a consequence, they judge the world by those standards and tend to make moral judgements about behaviors and the actions of others.

> They have great self control and seek to be effective team players.

LESS VALUED:

> Such individuals tend to march to their own drum, and they base their decisions on their personal reactions to given situations and people. They hate restrictions or rules which limit their freedom in any

way. They also resist it when others try to impose rigid codes of behavior—in turn, they never try to impose their behavior code on others. In fact, they don't feel any responsibility for the behavior of others. They are true individualists.

INTERACTION
STRONGLY VALUED:

Altruism motivates those who place a great value on interaction, and they have a tendency to help others (friends or strangers). In fact, they go out of their way, invest both time and money, to improve the lot of others. They also tend to get involved in "causes." Their idealism affects every facet of their lives.

Social injustice infuriates them and impels them to act. They base their judgment on subjective data and their emotional response to the state of people or situations which create conflict for others.

LESS VALUED:

Unlike those who place a high value on interaction, these people are inclined to believe that each person profits in direct proportion to his or her own efforts. Hence, if someone is not doing well, they believe that is can be altered through personal effort.

They are not likely to undertake causes which are designed to help the underdog, but they may well set up a system by which others can profit if they take advantage of it.

Others may see their behavior as lacking in compassion, but that is not the case. They give each person the respect of believing in them.

CONTROL
STRONGLY VALUED:

People who place a high value on control are often ambitious, enjoy moving up the organizational ladder, seek individual power and status, and are excited by influence. They couple these interests with a willingness to take the negatives that come from such behavior. They believe that the prize is worth the price and are natural leaders who orchestrate meetings and rally support whenever they wish or need.

LESS VALUED:
> Those who place less value on control do not see pain and adversity as a good exchange for gain. They prefer to avoid the risks that the quest for power brings, and they avoid situations or people they consider to be undesirable. They will—however—work quietly behind the scenes to insure the success of their own causes.

Our values set the standards by which we live and operate, and they are the patterns by which we select our life style, our friends, and our goals. Therefore, it is critical that we understand not only our own value system, but also those of the people with whom we interact in business or in our personal lives.

Of what importance is this to the business world? A GREAT DEAL OF IMPORTANCE. Many of the most expensive and frustrating organizational and developmental problems are the direct result of clashes—or, at best, differences—of opinion or values. These clashes are seen in

- management/staff
- management/management
- government/educational institutions
- government/industry

and when they exist, productivity drops and with it—
in many instances—profit.

Business draws upon diverse and complex human
resources, and it is unreasonable to believe that those
who come from varied backgrounds and heritages will
automatically blend into a functioning, matched team
without some effort on management's part.

Families are not matched sets even though they may
well have similar physical characteristics. Even those
living in the same family and interacting with the
people over a lifetime still interact differently. Each of
us dances to a slightly different tune, and this patterns
our interaction. Thus, families shape and form because of the values of those who make up the family
structure. Tensions can be created or harmony enhanced by the way we recognize and deal with the
difference.

Our heredity provides us with the clay, and the environment shapes it. Our self-concept is our view of self,
and our personality is the world's view of us. No one
can doubt that the whole is literally a sum of its parts.

> ## KEY POINT # 4
>
> **Our values guide us, and our attitudes—whatever they may be—are an out-growth of our values system.**

PREVIEW POINTS

Compatibility is not an accident. It takes work, an understanding of people, a willingness to adjust to the needs and behavioral styles of others, but if you want to take the time and make the effort, the benefits are astounding.

5

THE ART OF
COMPATIBILITY

The art of compatibility requires that you be able to adjust your behaviors so that they do not clash with others. In order to do this effectively, it is necessary to know and understand behavioral types with which you must deal. As Shakespeare said, "Each man in his time [must play] many parts, " and T S Eliot stated this another way, "We put on a face to meet the faces that we meet." He was stating what most of us already know—we adjust to the situations and people we encounter in order to improve relationships—business and personal. If no changes are made, there is a predictable level of compatibility.

Studies have shown that we choose—consciously or unconsciously—to project an image to the world, and we shift that image to fit the situations encountered. In addition, we have latent behavioral patterns (styles) that appear when we are under stress or pressure, or even when we are relaxed. The world then learns to know us by both our projected images (styles) and those latent ones that appear from time to time surprising others and even ourselves.

Our research led us to identify six styles of behavior which combine and recombine into some twenty-two. Before you read the comments below, you may want to turn to the back of this book and take SELF CHECK in order to determine the style or styles that you share with the world.

The six styles are labeled:

> **LEADER** (Franklin D. Roosevelt would be a good example of a LEADER.)

> **PERSUADER** (Presidents Reagan and Kennedy represent PERSUADERS.)

> **PATIENT** (President Carter was a true PATIENT.)

> **CAREFUL** (Henry Kissinger exemplifies the CAREFUL.)

> **RESERVED** (Katherine Hepburn is a high visibility RESERVEDperson.)

> **INDEPENDENT** (Steven Jobs, the founder of Apple Computer, is typical.)

It is important to remember that any of these styles can assume an authority role, but each will approach that role in a very different way according to personal needs and motivators.

Remember the style your SELF CHECK answers indicated you were? Well, with that in mind, read on.

SO YOU ARE A LEADER

It is important for you to realize that the majority of the people whom you encounter will NOT be of your same behavioral style, and many will not be able to relate to your high drive for results nor your direct, straight-forward approach.

You will get along with

- a LEADER about 47% of the time.

- a PERSUADER 57% of the time.

- PATIENT person about 98% of the time.

- a CAREFUL person about 57% of the time.

- a RESERVED PERSON will be compatible with you about 47% of the time, and

- an INDEPENDENT (who is very much like you in many ways) will relate well with you only about 37% of the time.

What we want to do is change those percentages—improve them, and increase compatibility, and when you understand their reactions and yours, this is possible.

HOW CAN YOU COPE

WITH ANOTHER LEADER?

When you encounter another LEADER, you need to realize that each of you is going to want to be in control, so adjustments are going to have to be made in an equitable fashion if you are to get along. However, since both of you prefer to work with those who are businesslike, straight-forward, and deal in facts (not feelings), you will find it simple to move forward on projects. This is particularly true since you both want results, respect, and action.

WITH A PERSUADER?

PERSUADERS are also fast-paced people, but they differ from you in that they want a more sociable approach to interaction and are more inclined to be impulsive than is your nature. You will need to take time to listen and give feedback on accomplishments and progress because of their need for the recognition which that connotes.

THE ART OF COMPATIBILITY

WITH A PATIENT PERSON?

PATIENT PEOPLE move at a much slower pace than you do, and they need the security of clearly defined goals and guidelines. You will need to remember to give them time to consider new ideas and changes since they prefer to hold on to the status quo until a review of the pros and cons have revealed that the new direction is a safe one.

WITH A CAREFUL PERSON?

Although you loath details, CAREFUL PEOPLE are very comfortable with them, and are likely to be both cautious and perfectionistic. You will need to remember this and provide them with the security of knowing that what is asked is reasonable and safe. You will get along well when it comes to commitments and manner—they keep their commitments and prefer a businesslike approach just as you do.

WITH A RESERVED PERSON?

Those who are RESERVED feel as you do about small talk—it is a waste of time, and they prefer to deal with ideas and concepts. You will need to note that they work best when they have time to analyze the project and determine the extent to which it is logical and sequential. These individuals are also self-starters (so are you), but they may well prefer to work alone. Their basic shyness prevents them from letting you know what they are thinking, but it may also promote a manner that seems blunt, but businesslike.

WITH AN INDEPENDENT PERSON?

Those of this style, INDEPENDENT, are very much like you in that they are fast-paced, need to be in control of their world, and are quite willing to assume authority and all of the pain and glory that goes with it, but they differ in that they are more likely to challenge authority, run according to their own dictates, and challenge the establishment. You are comfortable in the establishment, but both of you will need to realize that your high power approach to everything may cause a collision if you don't determine a way to work mutually toward a goal or goals. You can't both be in charge simultaneously. INDEPENDENTS never see a roadblock—only untapped opportunities, and, like you, they love a challenge.

SO YOU ARE A PERSUADER.

Like the LEADER, you need to realize that your particular behavioral style is unlike that of the majority of the world. As a consequence, others may find it difficult to understand you at times, and you them.

People are the KEY to your success, survival, happiness, and security. This means that you work best when you are not alone. Because you do want to help others, interact successfully with them, and be in win/win situations, you will find the following information most helpful.

Remember there are two levels of compatibility—business and personal, and the information needs to be utilized in both situations. If you make no effort to adjust to the style of the other person, you will relate well with

- a LEADER about 56% of the time.

- another PERSUADER about 20% of the time, although it is far higher in your personal life.

- a PATIENT PERSON about 100% of the time.

- a CAREFUL PERSON about 65% of the time.

- a RESERVED PERSON about 56% of the time, and

- an INDEPENDENT about 47% of the time.

HOW CAN YOU COPE

WITH ANOTHER PERSUADER?

Both of you demand attention, and it is essential that provisions be made to meet that need. In addition, since both of you are not time-conscious, you may tend to get more interested in the people aspects of projects than in the detail ones, and this could be a problem.

Your enthusiasm and eagerness to move on projects may cause a problem unless you both pause and REALLY listen to what is being said. You both need to take time to get acquainted, and you both need recognition for what you accomplish. Take time for both. In addition, you both tend to overbook your time and strive to do more than is humanly possible in a 24 hour day—so it is essential that you take time to plan before acting.

WITH A LEADER?

Since LEADERS are far less emotional and enthusiastic than you tend to be, stress results and have the facts to back up your suggestions, comments or observations. Keep your personal life out of the conversation or situation. Let the LEADER be in charge—one way to satisfy you both is to have you select three alternatives and ask the other person to pick one.

Since you are both fast-paced and want action, there should be no conflict here, but you may be offended by the blunt approach and direct manner if you incorrectly assume that it is personal. If you pay the LEADER a compliment, make certain this it is related to tangible accomplishments.

WITH A PATIENT PERSON?

You will need to slow down when you work with PATIENT PEOPLE since they need all of the details and want all of their questions answered. Never push or rush these individuals, and do remember that they will want time to think about your proposal—its pros and cons and its security.

Take time to get to know them, and don't move into a personal relationship as fast as you often do. They are team players, and it is very likely that they will strive to insure that there is harmony and a smooth-moving operation.

WITH A CAREFUL PERSON?

When you are dealing with a CAREFUL PERSON, you will need to provide them with details, pros and cons, and plenty of time to think about all of it. In addition, they will be most likely to accept new ideas or change if they are part of the process, so slow down and let them in on it. NEVER SURPRISE them.

They are often perfectionistic, and you don't like details, so it can make a great combination or it can be disastrous. You may tend to ignore details—if so, that will upset them, but if they are in charge of taking care of the details, they will be done right.

You are basically a very outgoing person, but it will be better if you remember that they are turned off by emotionalism, flamboyant behavior, and those who are too friendly.

WITH A RESERVED PERSON?

RESERVED PEOPLE work happily alone on projects that require logic—so give them the emotional and physical space needed. If you are too outgoing, you will turn them off, so you need to respect their need for privacy—emotional and physical. If you are too inquisitive, they will be very suspicious of your motives. Once they feel that their personal world has been invaded, you will have difficulty rebuilding the communication bridge, for they will build a wall.

Never rush such individuals, don't be put off by their basic shyness (which some call aloofness), and be aware of the time they need—provide it.

WITH AN INDEPENDENT PERSON?

Like you, they are fast-paced people, but unlike you, they need to be in control of their world!!! Be aware that they may well charge straight ahead, state their points bluntly, and give abrupt instructions. They also tend to challenge and debate points. None of this is personal in nature, just related to their need to get things done and their lack of awareness of how you may react to the approach.

They march to their own drum and do not need the approval of the world, so if you don't like what they are doing, withholding approval will have little impact.

SO YOU ARE A
PATIENT PERSON

You are one of those who make the "world go round." You provide the stability and consistency so vital to the development of families, organizations, and companies.

Your style makes it difficult for you to understand the fast pace of others—in fact, it may disturb you at times because it is almost overwhelming to have to deal with those moving at breakneck speed through projects and tasks.

You are a natural team player and get along with almost everyone, but it is still important to realize that there are some adjustments that need to be made in order to maximize your compatibility levels. However, if you make no adjustments whatsoever, you will still relate well with

- LEADERS at least 89% of the time

- PERSUADERS 100% of the time.

- other PATIENT PEOPLE about 65% of the time.

- CAREFUL PEOPLE about 65% of the time.

- RESERVED PEOPLE about 57% of the time, and

- INDEPENDENT PEOPLE about 79% of the time.

HOW CAN YOU COPE

WITH OTHER PATIENT PEOPLE?

You must realize that they, like you, need time to consider issues before making decisions, and this means that they can not be rushed.

Friendships are important to them, and they enjoy having their efforts praised and appreciated, so mental support and appreciation are necessary. Don't bottle up your feelings, it will be a better relationship if you state your views calmly, in an organized way, and with the support that will prove your point.

You, and they, put great importance upon the welfare of your family, so try not to push them into activities that will take time or energies away from this important component of their lives.

WITH A LEADER?

These businesslike people prefer to work with others who are businesslike, fast-paced, and efficient. Their "bark" is far worse than their actions, and even when they challenge you or your actions, remember to maintain your dignity—if you don't, you will lose their respect.

Let them be in charge, but do stand up for your own position and/or opinions, and deal in facts—never emotions.

WITH PERSUADERS?

You will want to take time to get to know the PER-SUADERS, notice what they wear and do, and give them the recognition they need for both. They do not have the same sense of time that you do, so don't be surprised if they are not as punctual as you are nor as concerned about deadlines. They tend to overextend themselves. Many times this gets in the way of their promptness, but they do want to help and will go out of their way to do so.

WITH CAREFUL PEOPLE?

CAREFUL PEOPLE are even more detail-conscious than you are, and they will want to know all the details and pros and cons before any action is taken. You need to remember that they are very rule-conscious and that they will live by the rules and regulations set forth.

They enjoy maintaining the status quo, but if change is necessary, it is wise to have them as one of the change agents.

WITH RESERVED PEOPLE?

Because you seem to relate well to most people, you will understand that those who are RESERVED prefer to avoid small talk, do not like to be called by a nickname (except by close friends and family members), and have difficulty expressing their emotions or reactions.

They are logical, deal well with ideas and concepts, and are generally effective in their undertakings, but do not expect them to communicate freely with you, and NEVER invade their privacy.

WITH INDEPENDENT PEOPLE?

Your natural diplomacy may be sorely tested at times when you deal with independents who tend to be direct, blunt, and demanding of direct communication. They expect to have you tell them "like it is," and they will do the same for you—for they are results-oriented and move fast at everything, even communication. They WILL NOT by pushed, hate to have demands placed upon them (they feel trapped), and since they do not like to work under close supervision, they may well not give you any even when the occasion seems to warrant it.

SO YOU ARE A
CAREFUL PERSON

Because you care, many projects get done with a high degree of precision which if left to another would not have the level of accuracy upon which you insist.

You need to realize, though, that care and precision are not basic to all, and although this may annoy you—or puzzle you—it is important to understand and adjust for that fact. There are other areas in which you differ, too, and if you make no adjustments for interests, needs, reaction patterns, or communication styles, you will relate well with

- LEADERS about 57% of the time.

- PERSUADERS about 65% of the time.

- PATIENT PEOPLE about 65% of the time.

- other CAREFUL PEOPLE about 65% of the time.

- RESERVED PEOPLE about 57% of the time, and

- INDEPENDENTS about 47% of the time.

HOW CAN YOU COPE

WITH OTHER CAREFUL PEOPLE?

You need to remember that they also need details, precision, accuracy, and guidelines. They may also be perfectionistic, so you may want to tap these mutual strengths to insure the best possible outcome.

Both of you tend to strive for tact but be careful that this does not inhibit real communication. Also, you need to know that both of you have slow fuses, but you will eventually blow if you are pushed far enough. There will be no problem with commitment—you both strive to keep your appointments and live by your agreements, and neither of you forget when agreements are not kept.

WITH PATIENT PEOPLE?

Although you have many characteristics in common with PATIENT PEOPLE, there are some areas that differ markedly. Whereas they enjoy chit chat, you may not, and although they are traditional, you may be more casual in your approach.

Don't be surprised to find that they are quite possessive, want clearly defined job descriptions, and—like you—want the security of clear-cut guidelines, minimal change, and the continuation of the status quo.

WITH RESERVED PEOPLE?

Both you and those who are RESERVED tend to keep chit chat down to a minimum, and although you are both good with precise approaches and details, they are more likely to enjoy working alone in situations which give them the space to do it their way.

Although you are both good with structure, you approach the work differently. You enjoy tools, instruments, and machines, whereas they prefer to work with concepts and ideas.

It is interesting to note that CAREFUL PEOPLE are also often seen as RESERVED since they may well utilize both styles.

WITH INDEPENDENT PEOPLE?

Your style and that of the INDEPENDENTS are poles apart. You will need to "step cautiously since your styles are literally foreign to each other. Their manner is often blunt and direct whereas you strive for tact. They are often in fast motion and react negatively to roadblocks, whereas you prefer to move at a more deliberate pace. You run by guidelines and rules, they dislike restrictions. You are good with details, and they abhor them.

WITH LEADERS?

In some respects, LEADERS are like INDEPEND-ENTS, so listen carefully, strive to speed up your pace, and be business-like in your approach. Set time limits for projects—they are more concerned with RESULTS and PROCESS, so don't make it obvious that you weigh each decision. They believe in a quick assessment and a fast decision followed by instant action. NEVER belabor details when working with them.

WITH PERSUADERS?

PERSUADERS are also fast paced and have difficulty slowing down or tolerating a slow approach to anything. They have excellent intentions, but their love for others and willingness to help out may well lead them to overbook their time.

This same love for people means that they "collect" them, so don't be surprised or annoyed if they appear to name drop—they are just sharing. Since they need interaction, things will move much more smoothly if you will take time to establish a personal relationship with them.

If specific patterns or approaches are needed, MAKE CERTAIN that the guidelines are clearly explained in writing—they tend to move fast and ignore details otherwise.

SO YOU ARE A RESERVED PERSON

You are one who truly enjoys working with ideas and concepts and may well prefer to work alone in many instances. Others sometimes have difficulty understanding that you are not really aloof, just reserved. Your basic tendency toward shyness may add to the misunderstanding.

Because you are so different from others, you will find communication easier if you learn more about those styles. If you make no adjustments or allowances for the differences in styles, you will relate well in business with

- LEADERS 47% of the time.

- PERSUADERS 56% of the time.

- PATIENT PEOPLE 57% of the time.

- CAREFUL PEOPLE 57% of the time.

- other RESERVED PEOPLE 57% of the time.

- INDEPENDENT PEOPLE 57% of the time.

HOW CAN YOU COP E

WITH OTHER RESERVED PEOPLE?

It is highly likely that they also enjoy working alone on projects involving ideas and concepts, and you will probably understand their need for privacy. Since you both appreciate a businesslike relationship without chit chat or overly inquisitive approaches, you will probably to do well with each other.

Remember don't rush them—they also need time to think things through logically and sequentially.

WITH LEADERS?

You will need to recognize the fact that you run on a "different track." You may well need to speed up at times if the projects involve them, and you need to remember that they love a challenge—even in conversations.

Don't be upset if they are overly direct and realize that they want ACTION YESTERDAY. When a problem is given thorough consideration, they may well become annoyed.

WITH PERSUADERS?

PERSUADERS need to talk things out, and you may need to hold your own reactions in abeyance and LISTEN. If their enthusiasm overwhelms you, try to understand that they really feel that excitement. They have a need to be your friend, so be willing to take some time with them. Their need for a personal relationship may cause them to cross invisible boundaries that you have set up around your own personal life. If so, try to understand that their eagerness is not intended to upset you—it is just part of their joyful approach to life.

Be aware of the fact that they may well overcommit—try to fit into 24 hours what needs 48, so details sometimes slip past them—give them follow-up in writing.

WITH PATIENT PEOPLE?

In many ways you are like this group. They, too, need time to think, are analytical, and tend to prefer working on long range assignments in a thorough way with closure as a possibility. They do not adjust well to abrupt change, but may well be effective as one of the change agents.

They differ from you in that they are more sociable, and will take time to visit with their colleagues, not just their close friends.

WITH CAREFUL PEOPLE?

Both you and those who are CAREFUL avoid chit chat and tend to keep your interaction on a business-like basis. However, CAREFUL individuals tend to interact somewhat more than you do and are more likely to approach tasks from a detailed, perfectionistic view rather than looking at the bigger picture as you might.

Like you, they are good with structure, but they are less likely to enjoy dealing with concepts and ideas. There will be times when others identify them as reserved, but they are not. They have a wider social base, are less concerned with their privacy, and tend to want more support than you.

WITH INDEPENDENT PEOPLE?

INDEPENDENT PEOPLE are also idea people, and they can be very creative in their approach to problem solving. They move at a fast pace all of the time— whereas you tend to adjust your pace to the situation—

and they hate to be slowed down by details, people, or rules.

You will have to work on building communication channels—they do not automatically have them in place, but they are always interested in innovative ideas and challenges.

SO YOU ARE AN INDEPENDENT

You are truly "your own person," and you move rapidly toward any goal that has become important to you. You are also impatient with those who move less quickly and with routine assignments or detail work. Others do not feel as you do, so it is important for you to understand them.

If you make no adjustment in your own style to accommodate the styles of others you will relate well with

- a LEADER 37% of the time.

- a PERSUADER 47% of the time.

- a PATIENT PERSON 79% of the time.

- a CAREFUL PERSON 47% of the time.

- a RESERVED PERSON 57% of the time.

- another INDEPENDENT PERSON 37% of the time.

HOW CAN YOU COPE

WITH ANOTHER INDEPENDENT?

Since you are both volatile, it is wise to deal with another INDEPENDENT with great care, realizing that you both want to be in control of your own world, both hate details, and both have a tendency to steam roll toward your goals.

It is, therefore, a good idea to establish ground rules and agree to abide by them.

WITH LEADERS?

LEADERS are also interested in having "it their way." However, they are more likely to follow corporate rules and fit into a hierarchy than you are, but they also like to be in charge. Adjust! They are your corporate counterparts.

WITH PERSUADERS?

Listen to PERSUADERS, they need interaction if they are to be productive. They need time limits and help with their schedules—since they tend to over-book. They move fast, and like you, they are not detail people. They are sensitive, however, so take care that you do not hurt their feelings. If they are appreciated and supported as well as given recognition and an opportunity to advance, they will go out of their way to be helpful.

WITH PATIENT PEOPLE?

Don't become impatient with PATIENT PEOPLE, they need to have time to think things through, consider the pros and cons, and weigh the possible consequences and rules before they take action. If you understand that they like working with rules and time to be thorough and analytical, you are less likely to be upset by their slower pace and seeming possessiveness.

WITH CAREFUL PEOPLE?

You will find CAREFUL PEOPLE very much like those who are PATIENT. Rules are very important to them, and they also want all the details. In addition, time limits are important to them, and they resist being pushed and hate unexpected changes.

WITH RESERVED PEOPLE?

RESERVED PEOPLE are very thorough in their approach, and this is, of course, time consuming— something that may annoy you at times. However, they don't waste their time either, and they too rebel when someone tries to push them or force them to do what they don't want to do.

They are not people people, so don't expect them to function in highly social situations requiring a gregarious approach. They are too direct and straight forward for this.

Remember that a communication bridge is essential, and it can only be built when both parties are willing to interact harmoniously. You can help this process come into being by adjusting to the behavioral patterns and needs of others in your world—be it personal or business.

KEY POINT # 5

We adjust to the situations and people we encounter in order to improve relationships and our chance of interactive success.

PREVIEW POINTS

Everyone is a salesperson—we sell ideas, products, services, but all too often we do it without realizing that we are all in sales. Since this is the case, we need to be aware of our actions and their impact upon others.

6

SELLING IDEAS TO OTHERS

Everyone is a salesperson—we sell our ideas, our products, our services, but all too often we do it without realizing that we are all in sales. Since this is the case, we need to be aware of our actions and their impact upon others.

People buy the idea, product, or concept that fits in with their own value system and motivational base, and once we have learned to identify those, we can look at what we are offering or suggesting in light of how it fits in with that system or base. We also need to remember that people buy from people they like. Once the match is made and seen, the rest is easy. People sell themselves—it is just that some are more resistent than others because it takes them longer to see the need or fit.

The hardest lesson most of us have to learn is that we are responsible for ourselves, our actions, and the results we get. In the case of "selling" this is doubly true. There are approaches that can be made that will ensure success, and we can look at the world's super-salespersons and learn a great deal that will ensure our own PEOPLE POWER.

Why are some people able to "sell" any idea, product, or service, while others with dynamite products and ideas can't get others to even consider them. The difference? APPROACH. The good salesperson

- changes pace and approach to accommodate the other person.
- understands the importance of feelings and takes them into account.
- takes the initiative and then FOLLOWS-UP
- always follows-through
- makes a decision and then takes action.
- cuts through red tape when necessary
- gives attention to details.
- believes in the product or service.

If you will look at those who seem most successful in your world, you will find some common elements (and it doesn't matter whether they are successful in business or in their personal lives) and some common behaviors. If you want to achieve the same level of success, you need to learn how to use your strengths and skills and couple them with those elements and behaviors. No half-way measure for them.

- They know and believe in their product.
- They understand their position.
- They are enthusiastic about it.
- They are articulate in their promotion or support of it.

Enthusiasm is contagious, and knowledge is power, so they have combined two POWERFUL ingredients to put them in a POWER POSITION.

They are also PEOPLE-ORIENTED. You can only succeed when those around you are considered and their needs ar met. Those who assume that no consideration needs to be given to others, are really so single-focused (self-focused) that the base of success is being ignored. Man is a social animal, nothing we do is done in a vacuum—in order to exist, except as a hermit, we must interact over and over again. We must communicate, we must listen (not just pause), and we must build bridges to the others in our world.

Their people skills are honed by the fact that they have real empathy for others, they have patience when things don't go their way or when others don't immediately see the value of their views, and they are willing to change or adjust in order to secure their goals or further their projects. For example,

- they are considerate (i.e., the keep their commitments).
- they pay attention to details and understand their own position well enough to be able to answer questions patiently and fully.
- they are tuned in to themselves and others (i.e., they understand their impact upon others and are able to temper their tone or manner when needed).
- they are in control of their own emotions.

These people skills give them an edge over others, and when that edge is found in a self-assured, self-starter who is focused on results, that person has what is necessary to make a real impact upon the world and others TRUST him.

If you are not closing your "sales," you may be putting up your own readblocks. Let's take a look at some of the biggest ones, and make certain that you haven't taken an unnecessary detour.

Sometimes, we are too confident—we come across as a "know it all," and this manner "turns off" the other person who feels inadequate and "put down." The fact that three of the words in the last sentence are well-worn cliches reinforces the impact of the statement. The situation described is so common, that we use and reuse the same phrases to describe it.

There is no question about the fact that all of us need to be in charge of our own world, but when this need is carried too far and we become domineering, we find that barriers suddenly appear. We can't sell anything to someone who is busy "manning" the battlements."

LEADERS hate to be pushed because they sense a loss of control.

PERSUADERS resist controls because it limits freedom.

PATIENT PEOPLE resist because it takes away their time to analyze and weigh all facets of an issue, idea, service, or product.

CAREFUL PEOPLE feel a loss when pushed to make a decision or take action since often they aren't through collecting the details they need.

RESERVED PEOPLE react very negatively to "pushy sales" types.

The **INDEPENDENT** refuses to give up power to anyone though at times what is taken for a power play is really a fast pace.

We need to be insightful enough to read the behavioral styles of others and understand how they will react to given measures or approaches.

Maybe it would help you better understand what not to do if we outlined some of the things our research has shown us may well happen when certain behavioral types are trying to sell an idea, product, or service.

LEADERS are often so confident, or come across so confidently, that they create the problems noted. In addition, they may hate dealing with details so much that they skip preparing or expect someone else to take that responsibility. When this happens they may do all right with others who are results-oriented and fast-paced, but they are likely to encounter real problems when using this approach with a process-oriented person.

If they aren't careful, they will also move too fast, push for closure, and fail to tune-in to the other person's need to ask questions, have precise answers, receive recognition, or have some control over the direction being taken. Obviously, when any one of these things happens, the "sale" is likely to be lost.

PERSUADERS are also likely to skip details and move too fast with the same results, but there are other things that they may do that will also result in "no sale." Excitement is one of their virtues, and also one of their vices since they may be so excited that they literally talk the other person out of the sale. This same excitement is coupled with a love for people and a need to help or be involved, the results—overbooked calendars. This tendency to over-book may also mean that they put too many things on their calendars and have difficulty living up to their promises.

The other results-oriented style, the INDE-PENDENT, often collides because of a lack of patience. They feel drowned in excessive details, so they don't impose them on others, and their own desire to "hear it like it is" prompts them to tell it "like it is." The results—an overly blunt approach and manner which may offend or, at best, jar others.

Although the majority of the population falls into the detail-oriented category, the three styles that are part of this category are different in many ways.

The PATIENT PERSON tends to over-pre-pare, insist on clearcut priorities, and deal thoroughly with each facet of the idea or concept. Thus, they often fail to note when the other person is ready to "buy into" the concept or idea and miss out by going on too long. They also get side-tracked and take the other person on a detour that leads away from the point being made or the idea being pitched.

The CAREFUL PERSON also tends to over-prepare and then relate all of those details to the other party—this is great if the other person is interested but a real problem for the person who just wants the "big picture" but gets every piece of the puzzle whether it is wanted or not. Because we are all so different and have so many different needs, there is a real need for flexibility, but CAREFUL PEOPLE need to move forward in a straight line, and unless they can adjust and detour as needed, they may well fail to convice the other person of the rightness of a given idea or product. Also, unless their behavior differs from most of those in their behavioral style, they will back down when they should stand up and take an assertive position.

RESERVED PEOPLE are likely to treat you as they want to be treated. They only buy that which leads sequentially and logically to a given conclusion or position. Hence, they will supply details, answer questions, and do it all with an aloof dignity which may well fail to sway the other person. In addition, they will logically weigh the pros and cons of a given situation or issue before making up their minds.

Now the INDEPENDENT moves forward without concern for roadblocks—even you if you are there—tells it like it is, talks fast, and is impatient with those who do not make decisions quickly and easily. Those who need the details, want time to mull over issues, and need a little TLC, are not likely to buy product or ideas from this person.

Did you spot your own behaviors in the above descriptions? (Remember that most of us have more than one style.) Good! Now you know what can go wrong, but let's end on a positive note, and find out how to make that sale.

First, learn to recognize the other person's behavioral style or styles, and then make certain that you keep in mind the needs of that type and how you can meet them, how what you are suggesting or offering fits in, and how you need to let them know this.

Let's look at **LEADERS**. When you have an idea to present or a concept to sell, be

- **PREPARED**
- **BUSINESS-LIKE**
- **ABLE TO SHOW HOW WHAT YOU HAVE IS WHAT IS WANTED**
- **FAST PACED**
- **RESULTS ORIENTED**

On the other hand, if the person is a **PERSUADER**, be

- **WILLING TO TAKE TIME TO BUILD RAPPORT**
- **OPEN TO QUESTIONS**
- **WARM AND FRIENDLY**
- **MATCH THE FAST PACE**
- **MATCH THE IDEA OR PRODUCT TO THE PERSON'S DREAMS**

Now the **PATIENT PEOPLE** need to have you

- **TAKE TIME**
- **SLOW DOWN YOUR PACE**
- **PROVIDE DATA**
- **REMEMBER HOW IMPORTANT FAMILY IS TO THEM**
- **WORK WITH THEM AS A TEAM MEMBER**

The **CAREFUL PEOPLE** will insist that you

- **PROVIDE PRECISE DETAILS**
- **SUPPORT THE STATUS QUO**
- **ARE CORDIAL**
- **GET DOWN TO BUSINESS QUICKLY**
- **KEEP THE INTERCHANGE HAR-MONIOUS**

RESERVED PEOPLE are often very private people, and you need to remember that and

- **USE LOGIC IN YOUR EXPLANATION**
- **APPROACH EVERYTHING SEQUENTIALLY**
- **TAKE AS LITTLE TIME AS POSSIBLE**
- **BE BUSINESS-LIKE**
- **AVOID INTIMACY—EVEN FIRST NAMES UNLESS ASKED TO USE THEM**

Only five percent of the world are **INDEPEND-**

Only five percent of the world are **INDEPEND-ENTS,** but when you encounter them, you need to remember that

- **THE BIG PICTURE IS VITAL**
- **THEY NEED TO BE IN CHARGE**
- **YOU SHOULD PROVIDE CHOICES**
- **THEY CONSIDER IT FUN TO SHOCK YOU**
- **THEY CAN BE INTRACTABLE WHEN PUSHED**
- **THEY ARE OPEN TO INNOVATIVE IDEAS AND APPROACHES.**

It may seem impossible to remember all of this, but it is well worth the effort to do so. When you know what is needed and wanted, you are well on your way to achieving the real base of power—PEOPLE POWER, an understanding of the elements that make the difference in every aspect of life. You can't sell anything until you promote a need on the part of the other party, and you can promote that need when you know what is needed and what works. Do you remember the Music Man—he showed the people in River City where the trouble was and then provided a solution. You can do the same. Try it—you really will like the results!

KEY POINT # 6

People sell themselves on ideas, products, and services—some are more resistant than others because it takes them longer to see the need and recognize the "fit."

PREVIEW POINTS

Stress can be a roadblock to success or a stepping stone to creativity—the choice is yours.

7

STRESS: THE ROADBLOCK TO SUCCESS

S tress is truly a roadblock to success, and this is no less true in your personal relationships than it is in your business life. Some of us deal well with change, others do not, just as some people can handle risk while others panic when forced into risk situations. In other words, there is no one cause of stress, but there are a number of events which can impact upon you and result in stress.

A recent FORTUNE magazine study of some 500 CEO's showed that their mortality rate was actually 37 percent lower than that of the average person, and a Gallup Poll showed that only 19 percent of those running top companies even considered stress a problem Why? They approached what to others might be considered stressful situations as challenges, and that attitude made a difference in not only their approach but also in their reaction to the situation and its impact upon them. Our concern with stress and its negative consequences is quickly assessed by looking at the number of seminar companies that were offering programs related to controlling stress. In 1989, it was easy to find a program—almost every major seminar company had an offer and in-flight magazines (which cater to business travelers) had article after article dealing with the topic and product after product being offered as aids in the fight against stress and its consequences.

Those who feel a sense of purpose and commitment, those who view change as a challenge and not a threat, and those who understand the need to interact effectively, aren't negatively affected by stress according to Suzanne Kobasa, a stress researcher. Instead, such people use stress to sharpen their endurance and coping skills.

Stress unchecked leads to burnout, and many fail to cope well with the causes of stress and fail to recognize the stages leading to burnout. Yet, some positive action and pre-planning could turn stress from a negative force into a positive motivator.

What are some of the causes of stress? There are four major ones;

- no sense of direction (no goals)
- a need to compete (self or externally imposed)
- a feeling of isolation (no support system)
- poor communication skills and the inability to resolve problems through communication.

These causes can be found in both personal and business situations, and the stages that follow are also predictable. Many of us feel deep fatigue when our stress level builds, and with this feeling comes a decreased interest in socializing—which may well intensify the feeling of isolation and abandonment. As we withdraw into ourselves, we find it more and more difficult to get up in the morning and less and less pleasant to go to work (or in the case of children, school). As this rut gets deeper, we find our productivity decreasing, and our emotional and physical problems increasing.

Before major consequences are visible, however, we are given plenty of clues—emotional, physical, and mental, examples of which are shown below:

EMOTIONAL	PHYSICAL	MENTAL
Irritability	Fatigue	Boredom
Depression	Ulcers	Paranoia
Tears	Tooth decay	Fear
Wild laughter	Rashes	Phobias
Unfounded anger	Headaches	Cynicism
Mood swings	Backaches	Impatience

WHAT IS YOUR STRESS LEVEL? FILL OUT THE FORM BELOW AND FIND OUT! The point value of each item is in parenthesis next to it.

1. I have very supportive friends and family. (+ 10 points) _____

2. I have a "haven"—a place to go to when I need peace and quiet to work or think. (+10 points) _____

3. I have a hobby or a non-work related activity that I turn to on a regular basis. (+10 points) _____

4. I am good at handling multiple priorities and balancing my time. (+10 points) _____

5. I am concerned about health and make certain that each meal is nutritionally balanced. (+5 points for each one) _____

6. I take time for myself during the week—time out to do what I enjoy doing. (+5 points) _____

7. I pay attention to my weight and am within
   15 pounds of my ideal size. (+15 points)   _____

8. I know the value of stress reduction activities
   and make certain that I engage in them at least
   3 times each week (i.e., visualization, biofeed-
   back, relaxation techniques.) (+15 points)   _____

9. I exercise 30 minutes or more each day. (+105 points)
   six days a week (+90 points)
   five days a week (+75 points)
   four days a week (+60 points)
   three days a week (+45 points)
   two nights a week (+30 points)
   once a week (+15 points)   _____

10. I take something to make me sleep
    every night (-70 points)
    six nights a week (- 60 points)
    five nights a week (- 50 points)
    four nights a week (- 40 points)
    three nights a week (- 30 points)
    two nights a week (- 20 points)
    once a week (- 10 points)   _____

11. I bring home work every night (- 25 points)
    four nights a week (- 20 points)
    three nights a week (- 15 points)
    two nights a week (- 10 points)
    once a week (- 5 points)   _____

12. I need medication to reduce my anxiety and
    calm me down every day (- 70 points)
    six days a week (- 60 points)
    five days a week (- 50 points)
    four days a week (- 40 points)
    three days a week (- 30 points)
    two days a week (- 20 points)
    once a week (- 10 points)
                          TOTAL POINTS   _____

TOTAL POINTS _____

SCORING INSTRUCTIONS

Add or subtract points as warranted and then use the scale below to determine your current stress level.

80 points or above: You should be able to handle most stress effectively and without negative physical consequences.

60-75 points: Although there may be times when you find particularly difficult situations stressful, in most instances, you effectively deal with the stress you encounter.

60 points or less: Even trivial situations may put a strain on you and tilt you away from an even emotional keel. You should consider making some lifestyle, behavioral, or attitudinal changes.

ACTION THAT WORKS

SHORT TERM HELP

It would be wonderful if we could take an old-fashioned rest cure when stress builds, but that is seldom possible or even reasonable. What you can do is take some mini-vacations.

• Get up and move away from the location where you were when the stress hit. For some reason, our minds seem to anchor stress to locations. Think about it. You can probably recall locations where you are suddenly overwhelmed by remembered negative reactions.

• Take a deep breath. We can reduce the impact of stress this way since oxygen is a stress reducer. Lately, a number of in-flight magazines have been advertising small tanks of oxygen for the use of the executive facing a stressful situation.

• Visualize yourself in a place that to you is restful and serene. Hear the wind in the trees, see the colors, listen to the chirping birds. BE THERE! You will feel a shift and a lowering of tension even if you only do this for 30 or 60 seconds.

• Learn how to do muscle relaxation. Lie on your back and relax your muscles beginning with the toes on your dominant side (find which side is dominant by intertwining your fingers and clasping your hands. One thumb will probably be on top of the other—in most instances, that thumb represents your dominant side—left thumb on top; left side dominant. If you don't believe it, reverse your interlocking clasp—is it comfortable? If it is, you probably can do things with both hands. If it isn't then the other pattern represents your dominance). Once your toes are relaxed move on up that side and relax each muscle in turn—by the time you reach your shoulder, you may well be asleep.

• Get involved in a vigorous physical exercise routine—it results in marked stress reduction since the brain releases a chemical which produces euphoria.

There are some other approaches you can use that will also put you in charge of your reactions.

• Get involved in "challenge exercises." We can't tell you what will be challenging to you, but we can share an example of what works for others. Some people put what they have to do on the right, work on it directly in front of them, and then move it to the left when it is finished. They can thus get a "visual reading" on their progress. Find a system that works for you—and USE IT!

• Alter you daily schedule in some way. Most of us get up at the same time each day, get a hot drink (or whatever it is that we do first), shower, dress— even putting on the clothes in the same order, get in our cars (or on our bus) and go to work by the same route. When we get to work, we park in the same place—even becoming very upset if someone has had the nerve to park in our unassigned parking place—enter by the same door, go to our

---

desk and begin our day in the same say. Such a pattern contributes to a form of boredom, and boredom leads to stress.

- Find something you can take control over, because success breeds success. Success engenders a positive outlook which in turn promotes success—the cycle of options. For example, if commuting is a problem, see if you can go on flex time at work and thus avoid the most heavy traffic periods.

- Learn to delegate. Don't let others make you feel guilty when you delegate, and do not think that you seem less competent when you do so. Orchestrating delegated duties takes real organizational skills, skills of which you should be proud. Time is certainly a factor—if it is going to take more time to explain it than to do it—then by all means do it yourself. However, if the person will do it over and over again—take the time now to save time later.

- Get a support system (actually three). You need a personal support system (your own pity party/brag group—those to whom you can turn when you "blew it" or when you think you were FANTASTIC and know that they will be appropriately happy or supportive); a professional support group (a professional organization), and two mentors (one male and one female to get both points of view).

In addition to the things that you should do, there are some things that you should not do.

• Don't find someone else to blame. Take the responsibility for your own actions.

• Don't "gunny sack" your feelings—gunny sacks eventually become overloaded and explode. Share your feelings in non-emotional ways a little at a time.

• Don't give up until "it" is perfect. This is an attitude that puts your progress on stall. Be as accurate as possible, and then move on.

• Placate at all costs? NO. Learn how to be assertive. Assertive people stand up for their own rights while aggressive people step on the rights of others.

Your behavioral style is to a large measure responsible for determining which events will be internalized as stress and which will not.

Since this is the case, it is helpful to know the types of events which will cause you stress and what causes stress in others. The information below will help you learn more about you and others.

STRESS

LEADERS feel stress when
- they fail to get their point/s across.
- there are too many rules which can't be worked around.
- too much socializing is required.
- too many details have to be handled.
- there is too much paperwork involved.
- they can't be in control.

PERSUADERS feel stress when
- there is not time for socializing.
- schedules are too tight.
- there is no personal appreciation.
- there are too many details or routine tasks.
- others move at a slower pace.
- they have to work alone.

PATIENT PEOPLE feel stress when
- the pace is too fast.
- they have to put work before the needs of their family.
- when they are not appreciated.
- when they don't have time to be thorough or analytical.

- when data, people, or assignments are not consistent.

CAREFUL PEOPLE feel stress when
- there is a lack of structure.
- rules are not followed.
- too much personal interaction is needed.
- when people are late or do not keep their word or appointments.
- when they are not given the details.
- when there is abrupt change over which they have no control.

RESERVED PEOPLE feel stress when
- forced into group activities.
- they have to socialize in large groups.
- they can't work with ideas and concepts.
- they are involved in conflict.
- when there is unexpected change which seems illogical.

INDEPENDENT PEOPLE feel stress when
- too much detail is required.
- any attempt is made to force them into conformity.
- others ignore their suggestions or instructions.
- there is too much formality.
- they are told what to do.

Many stress studies have been done, but none has considered the role behavioral style plays. We do know, however, that when the symptoms occur, STRESS is in the power seat.

MENTAL

The mind is an integral part of the entire human system, and stress does not ignore it. Often under stress, people are known to forget things and complain about their memory lapses. Attention spans shorten and response time is slow. At such times, it is not unusual to have people suddenly turn into "nit pickers" who are also indecisive and disorganized.

PHYSICAL

The first step of stress invasion is generally physical, and when action is not taken to alleviate the problems causing the stress, other symptoms appear. Headaches are one of the most common complaints of stress victims, but skin disorders, stomach upsets, and high blood pressure run a close second. Flu and cold symptoms are believed to be activated by stress, and there is a great deal of evidence to indicate that stress-ridden people are more accident-prone and have more difficulty with various appetite disorders.

EMOTIONAL

When tensions mount, it is not unusual for family problems to occur, and depression is not uncommon. Irritability grows, and some people also become hyperactive. When any of the above symptoms are ignored, behavioral changes often occur.

BEHAVIORAL

Fatigue is one of the most common behavioral complaints, but recent reports on stress have indicated that increased tardiness, increased absences, and insomnia are also frequently noted stress-produced problems. It is believed that excessive drinking, excess eating, and excess smoking are easily identified stress clues. The person under extreme pressure is likely to develop other easily identifiable symptoms—compulsive behavior, drug abuse, erratic behavior, daily use of anti-acid, or workaholic tendencies.

If any of these symptoms is present in your life, look for the cause, try to note the symptoms early, for problems in the early states are often fairly easily corrected. Take charge, and learn to use stress as a constructive force which can help propel you forward. Take charge—to paraphrase a popular advertisement— you're worth it!!

When you see problems as challenges, you will find that you are more creative and far less stressed.

KEY POINT # 7

Many successful individuals use stress to sharpen their endurance and coping skills instead of letting it become a burden and an enemy.

PREVIEW POINTS

Anything is possible. Whatever the mind can conceive, it is truly possible to bring into existence, and one only has to look at such works as BRAVE NEW WORLD for positive support for this theory. By 1958, the date BRAVE NEW WORLD REVISITED was issued, most of that which Huxley visualized in 1934 (the publication date of BRAVE NEW WORLD) had come to pass. This is no less true in our own lives. Believe in yourself, visualize your goals as actualities, and claim them.

8

HARNESS YOUR CREATIVE POWER AND RUN WITH THE WINNERS

We once attended a lecture where the speaker said, "What ever the mind can conceive, the person can achieve." That may seem like a gross exaggeration, but it isn't. Consider these points

- we only use a small portion of our mental capacities.

- although the majority of the population seems to be left brain dominant, the right hemisphere is still the mysterious, artistic side where metaphors are understood and emotions are realized. This is the hemisphere where dreams and imagery occur and fantasies are born.

- we learn early that conformity and retention are praiseworthy, but being "different" is not acceptable.

What does this mean to us—it means that we have the potential to be highly creative, but we may not take advantage of that potential. If we can find a way to link our highly creative processes to our goals and aspirations, we will literally be able to bring about the "impossible."

If you want to tap the "mystery" side of your brain there are ways to shift your perception from left brain viewing to the right side. Since the left hemisphere controls analytical, logical and structured thinking processes while the right hemisphere controls interaction and creativity, we utilize all quadrants to varying degrees. By changing views, you can experience the physical difference between perceiving with your left brain and with your right, you can modify your approach to many activities.

TRY THIS:
Take a line drawing. Put it in front of you— right side up—and try to recreate it. (This works best for those who are not trained or naturally skillful artists) Set the completed drawing aside. Now turn the line drawing upside down and recreate it. Compare the two

drawings. The one copied from the upside down drawing is probably the most like the original.

WHY?

You bring a great deal of your left brain into play during the creative process of drawing, and that hemisphere judges, evaluates, and seems to control what the right hemisphere produces. When the picture is turned upside down, it is no longer logical in structure, so your logical barriers are down. Thus, you can duplicate without being inhibited by the more rational left hemisphere.

Now, how can this work for you in other situations— obviously, you don't plan to spend your whole life drawing?

STEP ONE:

Define a problem you have not yet solved or a goal you have not yet met.

STEP TWO:

Number from one to six on the left side of the paper and from seven to eleven on the right side. NOW—write down eleven excuses (reasons) why you have not solved the problem or met the goal.

You will probably put down three to five reasons right away, but you may slow down at that point. What we do is put down first—and fast—those reasons we have been giving others and ourselves. The rest of the eleven will be harder—BUT DIG AND FIND THEM.

STEP THREE:

Go back over the eleven and cross out those that REALLY ARE NOT viable reasons.

STEP FOUR:

Look at those left and try to find elements that they have in common. Write those down.

STEP FIVE:

Select one of those elements and design a game plan to effect a change and secure your goal or solve your problem.

HOW? — easy. Brainstorm. Remember that brainstorming means that you will jot down everything that comes to mind without judging it or assuming it can't work. (Try it—in the next 5 minutes jot down all the ways you could improve a common pencil [i.e., we could attach a homing device that would make it return to its owner if it were lost; we could have the last two inches made of a nutritious sweet so that children would gain from chewing on the end—which they seem to do anyway]). If you have trouble getting started, try going in reverse. For example, if you are trying to reduce turnover, you might stop and see if there are some positives to having it. It does reduce costs, it may allow you to bring in new people, it will give you access to new ideas. When you look at your problem in reverse it sometimes lets you see that you are moving in the wrong direction.

NOW, cross out the ideas that seem too "way out."

NEXT, Design the game plan. Include the 3 W's and an H. WHAT is to be done, WHEN is it to be done, WHERE, and HOW? WHO will implement it and WHEN, and WHO will follow up to make certain it happens? (See sample in appendix.)

There is no magical route to creativity—Edison indicated that his "genius" was 99 percent perspiration and only 1 percent inspiration.

There are a number of ways you can shape your thinking to insure success. Consider how you think.

- Are you a **future** thinker? If so, you plan ahead and strive to reshape your world and your role in it.

- A **past** thinker? If so, you dwell on the past and do not stress action now.

- A **present** thinker? If so, you function well in the present, but are a dreamer.

Also, consider your own self-talk. Those who say "should have, ought to, could have, might have, wish I had" are not building for the future but reliving the past. The only ideas that are being produced are negative ones—and they do not promote creativity or success.

Those who are preoccupied with the present see everything in relation to the present view of reality. Those who said the car would never replace the horse saw only the present; those who installed electric lights but kept the gas ones were also present thinkers; and, of course, the professor at Yale who saw no need for an overnight delivery service was wrong when he told Fred Smith that Federal Express would never catch on.

When you couple future thinking with brainstorming and effective editing, you have the foundation for a future gold mine (or mind). Remember the story of Coco Cola—a druggist developed a syrup which did not sell well, and he was not only willing but delighted to be able to sell that syrup to an enterprising entrepreneur who had another use for it. The syrup became the base for Coca Cola—a druggist with a great idea did not take it to fulfillment and someone else made a fortune that might have been his.

THE TIME IS NOW

As our world becomes more automated, there is a greater need for people who can operate in the CREATOR mode. We need people who can generate and implement ideas. The growing number of entrepreneurs and the increasing interest in cottage industry occupations indicates a shift in our thought patterns.

LET'S LOOK AT YOU

How do you generate ideas and what kind of ideas do you generate? Take a look at your own "to do" list—what does this list show? Are all of the ideas things you need to do right now (shop, stop by the post office, make a call), or are there some that are future goals? Is it a mixture of the two?

If it is not a mixture, what are you doing with your deluxe ideas—the ones that solve your problems and set your goals? Are there any ideas that give you direction; any that set you on a new path personally; ideas that will lead to new products or services? Sometimes we dream great dreams, but they never come to fruition. A very wise businessman once said to us, "on the plains of hesitation, bleach the bones of countless millions who, at the dawn of victory, sat down to wait...and waiting...died!" Don't join those millions. Just remember that there are four steps to success—

> FIRST you must be able to <u>visualize</u> what you need or want.
> THEN you must <u>want</u> it.
> NEXT you must <u>need</u> it.
> AND then with action you will <u>GET</u> it.

Only 2% of the population sets goals, writes them down, and then reads them regularly. Another 3% set goals, but never write them down, and the rest of the population-some 95%-just heads out hoping to get somewhere someday. Be one of the 2%—set your goals (short, mid, and long range ones),write them down, and read them once a day. This is a form of

subliminal advertising, and advertising that comes in
below the conscious level is highly successful.

Take time for yourself. Tune in to your own needs.
The harder you work, the more you need to relax. If
you are having difficulty fitting in relaxation time—
make this your first creative endeavor—find a solution to your lack of relaxation time. Define the results
you want, visualize them, and they are your's. If you
want something enough, you will take the steps needed
to bring it about. Also, remember to provide yourself
with your own "space." We all need a place that is just
our's, an activity that regenerates us, a "world apart"
to ease our tensions and our frustrations. In other
words—our personal therapy session from which we
can return refreshed and more productive.

Never break your momentum. There is a saying in real
estate—"Once you are on a roll, keep going, you can
vacation later." The same is true in problem solving;
once you are on a creative roll, keep going.

SOME TIMES ARE BETTER FOR YOU THAN OTHERS

What time is best? We all have a natural bio-rhythm
pattern. For a full week, watch your energy patterns.
Each time you have high energy, put a red check on
your calendar noting the time of day. After a week,

look back over your calendar and determine which period/s of the day are your high energy times. You will find that you are most creative and far more productive during those times, so plan your days accordingly.

SOME PLACES ARE BETTER THAN OTHERS

Most of us have certain places that mean certain things to us. For instance, the kitchen spells "work" for most women, and for this reason, it is important to learn to recognize the location, if any, where you seem to be most creative. Make a note of this, and plan your time to permit you to be in this location when you need a place to think and dream creatively. Where is best for you?

"Run with winners." We learn the most from those who have been there, who are idea generators, who are excited about possibilities, and who are alternative thinkers. You need to spend at least part of your time with people like these. Don't forget that **optimism** is contagious, but then so is **negativism.** If you spend your time with negativists, you will be vulnerable—it is easy to let them steal your dreams. Look around, find the opportunity thinkers, and make them part of your world—for your own sake and the sake of your creativity. Make a list of opportunity thinkers you know, and design a game plan that includes spending more time with them.

LISTEN MORE THAN YOU TALK — we all heard this adage as children, but it is very important for those who really want to harness their creativity and have PEOPLE POWER. Idea people are rich sources of inspiration, but NOT if you are the one who dominates the conversations. Most people are delighted to have the opportunity to talk to someone who is really interested, and if you will learn some interviewing techniques, you will find that the rich imagination of others' will trigger your own.

GET OUT OF YOUR BOX. Most of us are like Jason (a little green creature in a box). We live contentedly in that box until it feels tight, then we fight to find a way out of it, only to build another box that is bigger because we feel best when those walls surround us. GET OUT OF YOUR BOX!!! GET OUT OF YOUR COMFORT ZONE!!! Only then will you grow creatively. As long as you are totally comfortable, you are not stretching your skills or your creativity.

SET YOUR OWN DEADLINES. Remember when we were in school and many of our classmates put things off until the deadline appeared. Many of us still do this. So set your own deadlines, and really work to meet them. Don't let yourself become careless about meeting them just because you are the one who set them. Many creative people do this, and we wonder how they manage to be so prolific. Well, you can be too just follow Edison's example—announce your goal as if it had been achieved. Tell people that your book (or whatever) is going to be finished by such and such a date. You will hate to fall behind and not meet the announced deadline. **Believe it, and it can come true. Claim it and it is yours.**

BE AN EXPERT—get to know more about your field than any one else does. Be open to new ideas and then link them to what you already do or what you are planning to do. Will they make it more useful, more successful, more desirable? How? Remember that pencil? Well, begin to look at your own projects like that and then link the new to the known and used and get something that is even more exciting. Consider how that wobbly plane flown by the Wright brothers has been improved by people who would not settle for what was, but had to improve it. You can do the same—just begin.

SOURCES OF IDEAS—there is no magic well. There is only observation with insight. Let's consider that. Identify a need, be aware of what others are doing, and don't assume that all ideas are unique or new. They are just modified patterns of history. Even the scientists who worked with the atom in the 1940's were merely reshaping ideas that Lucretious had had centuries before when he noticed that "all things are in a state of flux, and if you change their relationship in that flux, you will change their external shape." This is roughly paraphrased, but is it nevertheless the basis from which the atom was split. Learn to be a builder—take what is and find new directions, new approaches, and new meanings. Look at what is and find new ways to use it. Determine what is needed and consider new ways to provide it and new approaches.

BECOME A METAPHORIC AND ANALOGIC THINKER. When you make an analogy of your problem and what it is like, you set in motion a new thought trend. Let's see what happens. Let's say that I have been having difficulty understanding my personal computer—it is awesome and a bit frightening to me. Well, my computer is like a giant file cabinet, and file cabinets hold information, they hide it from sight, they can't think for themselves, they don't provide me with any of their information unless I know which drawer to open or which file to look in. They are a resource, but not a "thinking" resource. I have to understand their system, or I can not get what I need from the. Now, if I will look at my computer as a giant file cabinet which will only give things back when I know which drawer to look in and which file to recall, I will be less intimidated by it. In addition I could write an instructional manual for children by visualizing this. Make them see the little man, opening the door for them, listening to them, and running here and there around the disk to find the drawer with the information in it and getting it, bringing it back, and putting it up on the screen. If they give the wrong directions, or if they give conflicting ones, the little man will just run in circles or sit down and pout.

NOW TO THE TESTING KITCHEN

Nurture your idea until it has form and substance. Now, "bounce it off" some of your most positive and creative friends. Get their feedback, be open, and take their ideas and add the ingredients needed to improve and polish them. PROTECT your idea from negative people, don't share it—it will be diminished in your eyes when they find fault, and many great ideas have never achieved their potential because they were shared with someone who drenched them in the cold waters of negativism before they could come to life.

YOU ARE IN CONTROL.

YOU CAN BE CREATIVE.

YOU CAN HAVE THE CREATIVITY THAT CONTRIBUTES TO PEOPLE POWER.

YOU CAN MAKE IT HAPPEN !!

KEY POINT # 8

If we can find a way to link our highly creative processes to our goals and aspirations, we will literally be able to bring about the "impossible."

PREVIEW POINTS

Just as there are various levels of management (highly structured positions are seldom managerial) there are also various forms. Influence, position , task, and personal charisma can all be the basis for authority in various situations and at various times. The needs and goals of an organization should dictate which is used.

9

MANAGING:
AN ART AND A SCIENCE

Power and management are often equated in our minds, and some positions and jobs have intrinsic power while others do not. For example, a general has power by the very nature of his position as does a parent, but a teacher has power only within the classroom although the entire fabric of education is dependent upon that control.

The more structured the task, the less power is built into the job. This is simple to understand. The more assertive the nature, the less structure is comfortable or can be tolerated. Those with highly assertive natures tend to move into power positions—positions which are not structured and give them the freedom of movement they need.

There are various levels of management, and various factors which determine the extent of the influence level of any leader. In some instances, influence is position based; in others it is knowledge based. Many companies find that "peer group" leaders are truly effective adjuncts to the managerial structure. In some cases, respect is accorded to the position—the "royals" of Britain; in others, the structure of the task itself provides the base for the influence. For example, if a bridge were needed, the person with the greatest level of influence at that time would be the one with the knowledge or the access to the knowledge to build it. The third, but the most important base of influence, is the relationship between the leader or manager and the person supervised or led.

In some companies there has been an attempt to "make everyone equal." When this is tried, it can be detrimental to the organization because with the diffusion of power comes a loss of power and, hence, a loss of direction although matrix management has met with some degree of success. In those organizations (and even families) where a quality circle approach to problem solving and decision making has been used, it has worked well as long as the ultimate authority does not abdicate his or her power and leave the "ship without a rudder."

LEADERSHIP AND POWER

The present social structure has led to a questioning of power, and with this questioning has come a new attitude toward power. It is no longer considered a "right" but rather something that is accepted only if it is needed by the development of the organization or the success of the task.

ANYONE CAN ASSUME AUTHORITY AND LEADERSHIP IF WILLING TO TAKE THE RISKS. There is, however, a difference in the motivation for that assumption. Each of the behavioral styles has the potential to assume the role of leadership, but the reason will be markedly different. For example, the three results-oriented styles (LEADER, PERSUADER, and INDEPENDENT) are all highly assertive, and they have an internal power structure which make it less necessary for them to have a power position in order to assume authority although they will seek such positions, too.

Such is not the case with the more detail-oriented of the styles, the PATIENT, CAREFUL, or RESERVED person, nor do they not need task structure as the base of their power since it is an internal guide for them anyway.

Now what does this mean in terms of leadership and management? Well, the LEADER has a great deal of built-in power and structure. If he had any more, he might be overpowering and, therefore, stifle creativity and cause resentment and defensiveness to develop.

The PERSUADER, on the other hand, is quite assertive, but has little built-in structure. In fact, when there is too much structure present, this person fails to function at the maximal level of productivity.

Unless cast in an entrepreneurial role, the INDEPENDENT finds it difficult to function as a manager even though he has a great deal of built-in power. The reason for this is that INDEPENDENTS are basically very powerful individuals who are very results-oriented. They make their own structure, but that structure may well collide with the values systems and structure by which others run. Since this is the case, they have to temper their basic instincts if they are to successfully assume a management position.

Acceptance is the key to management style of the PATIENT PERSON who may need to add position power and task structure in order to improve the leadership potential and success quotient. Although "acceptance" is a vital component of this style, it needs to be tempered, for it can get out of hand. They are natural team players, and this often gives them the needed acceptance, almost automatically.

CAREFUL PEOPLE create their own position, but they may need to couple this with the power of the position itself in order to get the results they seek. This is clearly evidenced in those instances where people have power positions which are easily identified by external clues such as a uniform.

Another group which has its own built-in structure is the RESERVED, but unlike the CAREFUL PEOPLE, they may not project this structure to others. Nevertheless, it stands them in good stead in managerial positions. They do better if the structure is coupled with a power position and information which can provide the base for a logical operation and sequential actions. It is also important to note that their structure is often the result of their ability to bring action to their ideas and concepts.

LEADERSHIP:
THE JOB OF MANAGING

A leader is a manager who can effect behavioral/ thinking changes. Anyone can manage things or products, but few can effectively manage people. The assumption of a leadership role is only the first step in managing. Successful leaders have traits that inspire confidence in the ultimate survival of a company or organization, they are self-confident, consistent, goal-directed, versatile, and couple a strong ethical base with a sense of urgency while creating an atmosphere of trust.

Since the majority of people seem to resist change and will prefer the known to the unknown, it is important to make certain that they are given sufficient reasons (and in the terms that fit their behavioral needs and style) to get behind your ideas and goals. They need to know why change is NEEDED, what will happen if the existing situation or problem continues, the dangers of NOT CHANGING, and the BENEFITS to THEM of changing. A very successful executive told us, "people will work harder, make changes, and produce more IF THEY CAN BE SHOWN WHAT IS IN IT FOR THEM." The critical key to good leadership is COMMUNICATION!

But before you can communicate what you want and need, you have to be the strategist. You have to be its architect, its implementer, and the leader who gives it the momentum needed. If you want to be a successful manager or leader, you must have

- the determination to "stick with it"
- confidence in your own abilities

- the energy to move at a fast pace and handle myriad tasks simultaneously
- the competence to;
- identify, analyze, and solve problems
- use effective interactive skills to influence,
- supervise, coach, control, and lead
- insure your own self-control as an actor rather than a reactor in times of crises.

As a leader you must enjoy the role of leadership, be competent in five skills, and able to use the right skill for any given situation.

- You must be able to identify a problem, consider its REAL causes, recognize alternative solutions, select the right one, and implement it with subordinate participation ONLY if needed.

- You must be the ultimate salesperson.

- You must know when to seek help and when to provide it.

- You must know when to delegate and be able to do it without over-supervising.

- You must be able to "read" your staff

in order to know which motivational package will work best for each one and then be willing to use it.

• AND OF EVEN GREATER IMPORTANCE, YOU MUST KNOW WHEN TO LEAD AND WHEN TO BE LED.

HOW WILL ONE MANAGE?

No one style has a monopoly on successful management. In fact, one style will have strengths where another will be weak. This means that once you have learned to read style, you can make substantive predictions about a given individual's ability to manage.

If you are dealing with LEADERS, you will note immediately that they have high expectations of their abilities and those of others. They will be on a straight course toward their objectives, and they will have difficulty understanding that not all people are as goal-oriented. Their approach is businesslike and bottom line, and they are self-starters who need to know that they have the right to move up as far as their talents will take them.

They are motivated by results, respect, action, assignments which are challenging, and affluence, and they may expect others to respond to these same motivators.

These natural managers, have areas that need work, too. Their dislike for detail, their tendency to move too fast, their blunt, straight-forward approach to communication can all get in the way of building a good rapport with their staff. They often need to pay more attention to the feelings of others, to details, and to adjusting to fit the person to whom they are talking or with whom they are working.

The warm and sociable PERSUADERS are always eager to please, people-oriented, fast moving, and willing to help or be flexible if the situations warrant. They are energetic individuals who work best with others who are also fast paced, but they will take time to help anyone who needs it. They care about people, and this is both a plus and a minus. It is a plus because they will take time to coach and foster talents of staff members, but it is a minus because it makes it very difficult for them to discipline an employee or take a firm, negative stand when situations call for it.

These managers need to interact, they are prestige and status-oriented, and, like the LEADER, they need the freedom to act on their own.

There are some traits that may get in their way. For one thing, they hate details and time constraints, so they often overbook their schedules and try to turn time into an "elastic" commodity. Their personal money management is not always the best, and their listening patterns may well need work. They do listen to people, but their interest in the individual is often so complete that they fail to hear all of the words, hence, they may well be accused of being poor listeners.

Since they are fast-paced, they sometimes become impatient with those who are not, and since they set high standards and goals for themselves, they may push others to the same levels. Although at times this may be good, there are other times that it will be a real barrier between them and their staff.

Managers who are PATIENT PEOPLE are often those most appreciated since they are natural team players who are both cooperative and task oriented. They want to have the time to be analytical, thorough, and time to do a thorough follow through. They work toward set goals, but are unhappy when there is a frequent shifting of goals.

They give others approval and clear directions because they want the same from those supervising them. They are also cordial, supportive, and provide the consistency that makes it easy for other detail people to function smoothly. They are not likely to set a fast pace nor be particularly assertive.

In fact, they will be more effective in their managerial roles if they learn to be more direct, less concerned with the details, and more concerned with the big picture. There is also a need for them to delegate more and be less time-conscious.

CAREFUL PEOPLE are effective managers when the guidelines for the divison are clearly set forth and when there is a standard operating procedure by which to run. They bring a time orientation and a precision to the job that makes them effective managers in departments dealing with precision work or details. Although they hate change, they can effectively bring it about if they are one of the change agents and not the receiver of abrupt change orders.

In order for the CAREFUL MANAGERS to successfully accomplish their tasks, they need a clear cut job description, clearly stated goals, a structured and orderly environment, and support and attention when appropriate.

Their tendency to be precision-oriented and highly organized makes it difficult for them to be tolerant of those who are not. Because of this, there is a need for this group to develop a more decisive approach, be

willing to take a stand—even stand alone when necessary—and improve their communication skills and
level of flexibility.

RESERVED MANAGERS are often those most difficult for others to work with because they are not
understood. These individuals are often very private
people who are idea and concept-oriented and very
able to work alone with little, or no supervision, on
projects requiring a logical, sequential approach. Since
most of us manage others as we would like to be
managed, they often state the points that need to be
made, deal with topics in a cool, detached way, and
expect others to move on into their projects with the
same level of logic and detachment. Those less
inclined to work in this fashion accuse them of being
aloof or cold. Also, those who are RESERVED find
themselves "put off" by highly gregarious people, and
their reactions may seem cold to the warm, outgoing
person who is everyone's friend immediately.

Since these managers want their own privacy, a straight
forward line of communication, and a logical reaction
to ideas, they assume that this is what others want.
They, therefore, listen with little emotion to the points
made, make their comments, and then give people the
time and space to work the problem out logically on
their own time line. Those who want more interactive
support, are thrown by this approach.

Thus, it is important to make certain that RESERVED MANAGERS develop the needed people skills, communication skills, tolerance (to make their job easier). and rapport needed to motivate their staff.

The entrepreneurial INDEPENDENTS are often strong-willed, assertive managers, who make a statement and expect to have action taken immediately. These fast-moving, results-oriented mavericks abhor details, and are unlikely to accept any roadblocks (which they see as detours anyway).

Money, power, results, and a challenge all motivate them, and they are likely to build similar motivations packages for others since they work so well for them. This is just one more reason that they need to learn people skills and communication skills and pay attention to the "real" message. Since tact and patience are two areas in which they often need help, it will make it easier for them to work successfully with others when they master both.

Despite the differences in each behavioral style's approach to management, there are certain common elements that are vital ingredients in all instances:

PEOPLE ORIENTATION—The real role of a manager is that of managing people.

RESULTS ORIENTATION—Workers do what you INspect not what you EXpect.

COMMUNICATION SKILLS—People work better, more harmoniously, and with less griping when they realize that their efforts are appreciated.

Be mature enough to admit when you are wrong.

A good manager listens as much as he or she talks.

REWARDS—With raises should go higher expectations. Not all rewards are monetary.

PEOPLE SKILLS—People perform best when led—not pushed.

FLEXIBILITY—No one is ever 100% correct. Learn from your mistakes.

ASSERTIVENESS—Decisiveness is the KEY quality of a good manager.

STAFF SELECTION—The right choice makes the difference. It costs more to

rectify a bad personnel choice than it costs
to be selective in the first place.

Managers will succeed if they remember that others
follow not because some mysterious form of leadership as been provided, but because the manager is
following them.

KEY POINT # 9

**Power is no longer considered a
"right," but something that is accepted only if it is needed for development of the organization or
success of the task.**

PREVIEW POINTS

The right choice makes a difference. This is no less true in our personal relationships that it is in our business ones. When the match is right, there is a definite success edge.

10

THE HIRING EDGE

The right people make a difference in every situation, and this is no less true in a business than it is in a marriage. When the match is right, when the requirements are understood, and the values of the business or partner match those of the incoming party, then there is a definite success edge.

In business, the interview is a critical point in the hiring process, and according to the Boston Consulting Group, "corporate behavior depends on strategy, leadership, organizational structure, people, and system...they form that elusive complex called, 'culture.'" The study upon which they were reporting produced information which indicated that the fundamental areas of a corporation require reshaping from time to time. The two significant conclusions of the report were that

- information and its analysis are valuable only when crystallized into strategy.

- corporate change stems more from changes within people than from changes within an organizational structure or system.

The choice of staff, its placement and promotional policies are the key factors in the success of an organization.

Since this is true, then there is need for a well-planned, skillfully organized interview process. Our work with clients has shown us that QUICK CHECK (the behavioral instrument that indicates drive, pace, interactive, and rule compliance levels as well as stress, tension, and/or confusion) and PEOPLE CHECK are excellent tools when properly used by the personnel staff. It is also important to consider many factors when judging the appropriateness of the person for a given position. No one measure is either fair or logical, but the following twelve can be utilized as a base with excellent results.

We suggest that you consider each of these and then weight it according to its impact upon the job under study. For example, in most instances health is not a major factor, but it is certainly a factor if the person is to be working with patients. Financial acumen would not be of concern if you were hiring a French teacher, but it would be critical to the functioning of a Chief Financial Officer. The total of the weighting process should be 100, and the twelve items should be considered with this in mind.

The areas are discussed in alphabetical order, not in order of any predetermined importance.

FACTORS TO BE CONSIDERED

AGE:

In most jobs, age is not a factor, but in some it is crucial. For example, there are positions that require that you be of the legal minimum age in order to perform the required duties. If that is the case, then obviously this will be an important item.

BEHAVIOR:

We often select people for jobs after checking educational background, skills levels, recommendations, experience, and interview impact, but we then fire them for things such as attitude, tardiness, absences, conflicts with other employee, etc. ALL displeasing behaviors. By using the proper assessment instruments, (we designed and use JOB CHECK,) it is possible to learn both public and latent behavioral patterns and related motivational patterns.

CHARACTER:

We generally depend upon references for this information, but VALUES CHECK, and other values assessment instruments, make it possible to determine the basic value system by which the person operates. This instrument will also indicate the positions in which the person would be most comfortable.

CONTACTS:

Most of the time this is given a very limited weighted value, but if one were hiring a lobbyist, it would have to be given greater point value.

EDUCATION:

> The educational level needed, or required, for a given job depends upon company policy, legal requirements, or corporate culture.

FAMILY FOCUS:

> It is important to consider this factor in some instances. For example, a job that required the person to be away from home a great deal would be all right with some individuals, but the basic behavioral styles and values systems of others' would make them far more family focused. In light of that, you might not want to place them in a job that required that they go alone to Arabia for two years—no matter what the pay.

FINANCIAL
ACUMEN:

> As was indicated earlier, it might be unnecessary to consider this for most jobs, but for a Chief Financial Officer it is a vital element.

HEALTH:

> The person needs to be well enough to get the job done. You might wish to check absentee records since time away from the job costs your company money and potential productivity.

INTELLIGENCE:

> There are a number of companies which use actual I.Q. tests, but there are many instruments available which are not in such disrepute. Those instruments indicate the brain dominance pattern/s of the individual. Our research produced BRAIN CHECK which we can administer in pen and pencil form or which can be taken at a computer terminal. It produces both a read-out and graph to help the personnel officer more effectively place and train.

INTERNAL
MOTIVATION:

> Our motivation stems from our value system, and by using instruments like VALUES CHECK, it is

possible to provide information on the six value areas (RBASIC— **research or truth, beauty, affluence, structure, interaction, and control**) If you understand what is needed in a given position, this information can provide valuable, related information.

PERSONAL
PROJECTION:

Each of us has about four minutes in which to make a negative or positive impression, and the skilled interviewer can use that time to pick up many important clues. It is even possible to "read" people with the help of computer programs such as PEOPLE CHECK.

For example, the person who walks into the interview in a matched and blended outfit, who speaks in a controlled manner, and who asks questions or answers them precisely will be good with details, have a system and need one, want support and time to weigh all of the data, and is likelt to be well-organized.

This person will support the status quo and resist change, and will want instructions to be full, detailed, and clear. Probably the wrong person for that high pressure sales job, but great for that programming assignment.

WORK
EXPERIENCE:

Recommendations and references give the information needed, but please remember that it would be highly unlikely for a candidate to give as a reference someone they thought would give a bad referral.

As an additional means of helping you make the decision, you need to know specifically what the job requires from a behavioral standpoint. Let's look at four vital areas in any position:

AUTHORITY
LEVEL:

Does this job require that the person in it assume a great deal of authority, assume authority only for the tasks assigned, or take orders at all points?

If this isn't clearly considered, then the person taking the job has no base for action, and it is unlikely that the right level will be automatically assumed—hence, dissatisfaction on both sides.

INTERACTION
LEVEL:

Often applicants are told that the job requires that they relate well to others. WHAT DOES THAT MEAN? Do they have to interact constantly as would a telemarketer? Be warm and sociable with a large number of colleagues? Be pleasant to people when they see them which is seldom?

If the secretary thinks she is to be warm and sociable and make clients feel good about calling in while the boss thinks that a brisk, short conversation is all that is needed, you can be certain that the phone approach will never fit the boss' expectations and the secretary will never understand why it doesn't.

PACE LEVEL:
> A fast-paced, results-oriented boss generally wants a staff member who is fast-paced. Actually, some jobs are best done in a thorough, careful way, and that requires a far slower pace. It is important to consider the job needs and not the boss' behaviors.

RULE
COMPLIANCE:
> The boss who hates details will probably want someone who can be a back-up. The research indicates that we should hire our **complement** and never our **clone**. In addition, the job needs must be weighed. If the job really requires a perfectionist, that needs to be factored into the behavioral analysis.

In order to insure that the best employees are hired, the above factors need to be considered, but it is also necessary to design interview and application forms that provide not only the "face" data but also the foundation information that helps the personnel staff determine fit. Such tools are available in generic form and can also be made industry-specific for a minimal cost.

Most good interviewers know that everyone has the potential to be a leader, but not everyone has the potential to be a leader in everything. So, appropriate placement is vital to not only the success of the company but also to the success of the individual. And since one man's strength is another man's weakness, the personnel should be not only matched, but also balanced.

When management remembers that it costs more to rectify a bad personnel choice than it costs to be selective in the first place and institutes a quarterly review system, fewer levels of management are needed, but the need for effective supervisors rises—a cost effective shift.

KEY POINT # 10

The choice of staff, its placement, and the promotional policies are the key factors in the success of an organization.

PREVIEW POINTS

Well-balanced teams take diverse talents and meld them into a cohesive unit. Thus, they bring to the problems at hand multiple approaches thereby ensuring the success of the undertaking and solutions that have everyone's support.

11

TEAMS: THE WAY TO GO

According to Lee Iacocca, any group needs to have both sides of an equation since the natural tension between two groups will create its own system of checks and balances. Such can be the case with teams if they are true teams. The talents of the team are geometrically multiplied to produce a unit far more powerful than any one of its members could ever be.

When a team which is balanced among the various behavioral types is assembled and when it represents the appropriate values and has the right amount of competitive and cooperative spirit, the job gets DONE. Because more than one solution is brought to bear upon the problem under study and different points of view are represented, greater productivity is generated.

Successful operations encourage people to go in new directions by using what is in essence an "invisible" leadership (the team of which it can truly be said that the whole is greater than the sum of its parts). Teams work successfully when the environment is conducive to it and when innovative ideas are appreciated and fostered. There are certain conditions that must exist if teamwork is to be maximized

- the team—not the individual—is rewarded
- the team develops trust
- the team is not over supervised

The idea of Quality Circles began in the United States, but the Japanese made them into a well-developed system of management. They learned the art of team building, found that it fit in well with their familial approach to business, and have used it to move ahead of the rest of the world in productivity, employee satisfaction, and high morale. Corporations—and even families—that use the team approach find that everyone can make a difference. In factories, blue collar workers are given the opportunity to discuss among themselves ways to improve or solve problems that are spotted during the daily work routine—ideas that have saved many thousands of dollars.

This approach works so well that now even top management has become involved in and actively promotes the concept of teamwork. It is not a new word, it has been bandied around for years, but words without a foundation of action have no substance. Initially, this movement was limited to the field of manufacturing, but it has now spread to the service industries such as banking, retailing, and restaurants.

The deadly tendency of many American managers—to give very specific directions and guidelines, has been avoided by those who opt for directions which open the door for imaginative, philosophical approaches to problem solving. Thus, mid-management has room to think, create, and explore new ways to reach old goals and new objectives.

Regardless of how the concept is approached, teams WORK!! For example, some companies encourage their workers to meet in small groups to plan and consider the implementation of those plans (television advertisements for one Japanese car firm have been built around this concept) while other companies—some major corporations—use meetings at which staff members are encouraged to make suggestions, voice concerns, and share ideas. One such company—Amway—is based in Michigan, and the monthly meetings are held with a stenographer present. It is that person's job to make certain that everything is recorded, and the manager's job is to follow-up, judge the request, concern, or idea, and then get back to the person and let that individual know the course of action that will be taken. No idea is too small and no concern too petty to consider, and from this interest in the individual and his or her ideas has come such minor changes as cafeteria offerings and such major ones as new, more distinctive packaging.

When clear-cut direction is involved in the planning for the use of teams, the companies benefit, and it is the purpose of this chapter to provide those guidelines, tips, and strategies which, if used, will make successful teamwork possible. It is assumed that the information in this chapter will be used in conjunction with that imparted in the other portions of this book to insure maximum productivity and profit as well as maximum staff satisfaction and motivation.

WHY USE A TEAM ?

There are many reasons for turning to a team to solve problems and produce innovative approaches and directions. Some are quite unique. Over a period of years, some major reasons have surfaced over and over again, and it is those which are set forth below:

COMMUNICATION:

Teams can be used to improve communication at all levels. All too often workers are expected to be dedicated to causes or projects about which they know little. We all perform best when we see value in our work and know how it relates to the "Big Picture." We need to feel worth and that is seldom possible if we do not understand the schematic.

PRODUCTIVITY:

When we are involved in the events and decisions which affect us and our lives and when we see value in our actions, our productivity increases. This is especially true when we can see how what is being asked or done fits in with our own personal goals and needs.

GOALS:

When we participate in goal setting, we are likely to "buy" into those goals and strive to insure that they are met.

USING TALENTS:

Within each company is a wide variety of talents, and often they go untapped—to the detriment of the individual and the organization. The team is one way to allow those talents to surface and to profit from them.

CHANGE:

In our work in corporations, we have found that about 70% of the staff is reluctant to deal with change. The status quo is cherished even when it is not liked, for many have difficulty adjusting to change. However, they adjust far more willingly and readily when they are part of that change—part of the body planning it.

MEETING NEEDS:

People need to be contributing members in order to feel commitment to an entity larger than themselves. It doesn't matter whether that entity is the family unit or the major corporation for which they work. Teams make this process possible.

OTHER:
　　　　When the "old" approach has failed.

When we contribute to and "buy" ownership of a
project or plan, we feel a sense of accomplishment and
also a sense of responsibility. With these two feelings
comes a feeling of pride and worth—two powerful
motivators. However, with those feelings comes a
need—the need for recognition of contributions and
accomplishments, and it is imperative that this recognition be given in order to maximize involvement.

WHAT CAN BE EXPECTED
OF A TEAM?

PROBLEM SOLVING is an excellent project for a
team. It has been found to be far more efficient to have
a group tackle a problem than to turn it over to just one
person who must take time to solve the problem and
then time to sell the solution. In fact, "decisions made
by teams are better understood and accepted by those
who must implement them."

When teams are used on a consistent basis, the groups
become more efficient and meetings begin to consume
less and less time because;

- members are more familiar with each other.
- intergroup understanding increases.
- competition decreases.
- there is increased interest in results.
- interaction and support builds.
- strengths are recognized, appreciated, and used.
- communication improves.
- mutual respect increases.
- the group process becomes more natural.

Of course, teams do have a life cycle—or should—since the situations change, the group dealing with the situations needs to change for a better talent/problem match.

There are qualities that make up a successful team, and these need to be recognized and team selections made in light of them: energy, persistence, creativity, people skills, objectivity, organization, communication skills, listening skills, and management's recognition of the value of the team approach.

USING STRATEGIES
THAT PRODUCE
SUCCESSFUL OUTCOMES

There are strategies that have been very successful in making certain that teams are set up to produce successful outcomes. When these aren't used, chance is the operative agent, and the team may or may not work.

The step is to set up a team, and it is best if members of this group are selected from a variety of division or departments. Thus, you insure the broadest possible representation, the maximal involvement, and a scope that covers all potential roadblocks, decide which divisions should be represented and determine the reason for using a team. If you need to have an innovative process developed and implemented, you will want to have at least one highly creative person involved. Every team needs a cross-section of behavioral styles.

LEADERS will take charge and orchestrate the operation. PERSUADERS will help the group build the rapport needed to operate and also will be able to sell the resultant concepts to others. PATIENT PEOPLE bring an analytical approach to the problems and have the ability to calm down those most agitated without losing their own "cool." On the other hand, we must have detail people who understand the rules and regulations under which we must operate, and CAREFUL PEOPLE fill the bill. The RESERVED PEOPLE will make certain that sequential steps are followed to a logical conclusion, whereas, the INDEPENDENTS will assume anything can be done—there are no roadblocks only temporary obstacles—and approach everything in a unique, and probably, innovative way. You need them all, but these diverse types need to be melded into a team.

You establish the term of operation, but it is up to them to decide direction, select the team members, and design the format and structure. Once this group is in existence, any member can pose problems for consideration, and each problem brought up must be considered from the point of view of the company's mission and plan.

There will be a need for effective communication, flexibility, group pride, and an interest in cooperative brainstorming. Once the team is on a project, there is also going to be a need to supply them with the support data and support staff necessary to make the problem solving process work and produce results. WHEN THE PROJECT ENDS, DISSOLVE THE TEAM.

THE TEAM LEADER

The team leader has certain responsibilities which make the difference between success and failure. He or she needs to get input from others, follow an organized plan of action, and remember that team decisions are an evolving process and do not produce overnight success.

Obviously leadership techniques are necessary, and the team members must be made aware of the leader's role on the team and in the company. There must be clear ground rules, and a union between management and employees is vital.

If this union exists, then the commitment and training needed will be provided, and although opposition will undoubtedly occur, success is possible. When high expectations are set, strong performance generally follows.

Now, the leader has certain things that need to be done and others that need to be avoided—a **do's and don't list,** in essence.

DO:

- be concerned about the task and the team members

- make decisions in the best interest of the company.
- be aware of—and accept—the differences among people.
- give recognition to the ideas and contributions of those on the team.
- be flexible.
- be aware of needs, resources, past actions, and the ultimate results sought.
- get consensus, not necessarily unanimous decision.

DON'T:

- avoid opportunities for innovative approaches.
- "pass the buck"
- run from conflict—resolve it.
- consider only the "safe" positions.

When this list is followed, the probability of success for the team and the leader is enhanced greatly. In addition, it is necessary to put each behavioral style on the committee. It is also important to know how to work effectively with each style. The following guidelines will help.

If you are working with LEADERS, you should

- establish target times and deadlines. They want to know the bottom line parameters.
- list advantages and disadvantages of the program plan in light of their interests.
- demonstrate through your actions—not your words. They tend to believe what they see not what they are told—especially if the two don't match.

Those PERSUADERS on your team will want you to listen to them and hear their ideas, but they will also work best if you are fast-paced and pay them compliments and give recognition when they have done particularly well. You need to make good eye contact, and remember—never rush them. They work best when rapport has been built.

Now the PATIENT PEOPLE will want your assurance, your personal attention, and work best when you are informal in your manner and slow down your pace. In addition, you sincerity is important to them, and you must be an active listener.

CAREFUL PEOPLE will remind you in many ways of the PATIENT ones, but they will want you to be even more direct, more specific, and give them time to make decisions after weighing all of the pros and cons.

The RESERVED PEOPLE on your team will insist that there be time to verify your words, your actions, and those of all other team members. At least this will be true until a level of trust has been built that removes you from the questionable category. When they ask for it—give support, get to the point, and be business-like in your approach if you want the respect and support of this group.

A businesslike approach is also wanted by the INDE-PENDENTS who want you to stick to the topic, state the bottom line, and let them make the decisions. If you want to have some input in those decisions, provide three choices from which they can choose.

There are roadblocks to successful planning, but when they are recognized, they can often be controlled or avoided. For example,

FEAR often blocks the success of planning of any kind—even that of a team. Fear of doing something wrong, fear of not having your ideas accepted, fear of assuming too much authority, or fear of making plans and then receiving little or no support for implement-ing.

CAN'T is a word that explains many failures. What we believe we can't do, we can't do, and all too often the attitude gets in the way of success. Those who believe anything is possible, it just may take longer, are often the ones whom we later say were lucky.

RESENTMENT also gets in the way of success. The reasons are varied—resentment of having to take on responsibilities others don't have to assume; resentment that we weren't put in charge, or were put in charge and don't want to be; resentment that our ideas were rejected at some point the the past and we are now being asked to run around that track again; resentment of the time the project is going to take and worry about how we can also get our own work done.

INFORMATION GAPS are often a problem Many times teams or individuals, are asked to take on tasks and complete them or solve problems when there is insufficient information available for them to make intelligent choices. Information is often doled out on a need-to-know basis, and such a process cripples truly creative thinking.

COMMUNICATION skills are needed to succeed in anything—particularly in teamwork, and the ability to match listening languages, "read" their styles, and adjust accordingly give team members a real communication edge.

SELF INTEREST may well get in the way of a team's success. If it is not in our best interest for this project to move forward or this problem to get solved, even if we are on the team, we may well use passive—or even active—resistance to insure that it does not succeed.

The SYSTEM sometimes gets in the way. There are many instances where people have come up with logical, effective, even innovative, solutions to problems only to have the rigidity of the system, the slowness of the system, or the structure of the system block implementation.

MYOPIC team members often fail to see the reason or need for a given direction, and when no need is seen (particularly when there is no personal involvement in that need), little is likely to happen.

What does all of this mean—it means that there are many roadblocks which can impede successful planning, and it is the responsibility of the leader to determine if some have been encountered, decide which, and figure out a way to do an "end run" around them.

DECISION MAKING

When decisions are made by a team, the commitment is far greater than when it is made by a cast of characters sitting in the front office and dictating from on high. There is actually a rising scale that indicates the "buy- in" factor—the decision least important in the minds of the majority is that made by an unheard "authority," the next in line is that made by a single individual, then the minority decision is next in line. Majority decisions have more impact, and group decisions come fairly close to team decisions in the level of implementation success. Obviously, not all decisions can be made by teams, but this scale needs to be considered and remembered as decisions are made within any organization or company.

Since people tend to pattern their behavior after their employers, business situations almost always come down to people situations. It is, therefore, important for those using teams to believe in them and select the people serving on them with care and for their styles and expertise. "People are blind to their potential; they neither know what is possible nor understand the rewards of self-actualization," according to Abraham Maslow. Through an effective use of teams, potential can be tapped, problems can be solved, and communication lines established which will be effective in all phases or work.

KEY POINT #11

Decisions made by teams are better understood and accepted by those who must implement them.

PREVIEW POINTS

The qualifications for success in the workplace have no gender base. Those who succeed demonstrate personal ambition and a commitment to the company and its goals and couple these with simple virtues—integrity, industriousness, and the ability to get along with others.

12

THE CHANGING WORKPLACE

There are well-established routes up the corporate ladder, and those at the top indicate that the three most important personal traits needed for success are simple virtues: integrity, industriousness, and the ability to get along with people. Those employees who succeed demonstrate personal ambition and a commitment to the company and its goals. These characteristics have no gender base, so they are no different for men than they are for women, but there are elements which do make a difference.

There is more and more stress placed upon the value of networking in the business world—it isn't new, just renamed. The so-called "old-boy" club was the base for networking for business' upper echelon for many years. The school tie was a symbol of far more than educational background. It was an indicator of status, entry into the "right" circles, and an interlocking support system. For many years, the best schools of business were closed enclaves—men only read the invisible sign. The first woman to enter Warton's "sacred" halls of learning came into the school in the late 1950's. In fact, those on campus at that time probably all remember when she caused a real stir at Lippencott Library. The library which is multi-storied is built with the center reaching up some four or five stories surrounded at each level by stacks bounded by rails. High above the central check-out desk was one student studying Moody's manuals. The new student—who just happened to be Miss Iceland—came in, headed to the check-out desk, and waited to be helped. The "serious" student in the stacks above leaned over to get a better look, and leaned some more to get an even better view—at that point Moody moved over to the edge of the rail where it had been balanced and fell from the "heavens" with a resounding crash—luckily missing everyone. Everyone looked up—then over to the desk, and laughter rang out—everyone knew who had done it, why it had happened, and agreed with his interest. Miss Iceland was truly beautiful and—of course—even more interesting since she was one of the first women to become a Wartonite.

She was interesting because she was unique—a woman on a man's campus. Times have changed, but not as much as we think. Let's look at some of the most recent statistics.

In 1987, it was announced in U.S.A. TODAY that 57% of all professional and managerial positions were held by women, but it was pointed out in several issues of magazines that year that only 2% of the real decision-makers were women. This will change, and there are more and more women entering the world of politics, medicine, law, and the technical fields, but the most interesting of all news is just now being noticed. Women are leading the world into entrepreneurial undertakings—they are starting a major portion of the new service businesses. As the old guard exits and the new guard moves up and in, there will probably be more and more women moving into the "large" corner offices of the corporate world (offices that Korda tells us indicate the real power positions). As Bill Russell once said, "Competence no longer is limited to one sex."

Many different factors have been, and are, involved in career choices, career placement, and career patterns, and studies have shown that often women and men see their careers differently. We have confirmed this in our programs—which have involved over 7000 people in the past two years—and found that women often see their job or career as a form of self-fulfillment, a means of promoting personal growth, and a way to make a contribution to others and their world.

Now, men want these things, too, but they also tend to see their career as a series of jobs—a progression that leads to an ultimate goal, SUCCESS and RECOGNITION. The last element has been appearing in more and more surveys filled out by the women in our classes in the last few months, but one speaker indicated that it had never appeared in any program she had conducted. It has been interesting to learn that most men do not separate job and career, but many women do. One woman said that to her a job was an occupation that took care of her needs right now while a career was her goal for the future, and when she enters it, she will know she had arrived. In a sense, this is what many students feel about their part time jobs which they take while they prepare for the future.

The growing shift in single vs. married status has altered one view held until quite recently. Men grow up expecting to support themselves and families, if they have them, for life; women used to grow up thinking that they would work until they married and began to raise a family. That view is not as common now on either side. More and more men look forward to a family unit in which both spouses work, and many women expect to continue working after marriages. This shift is having an impact in other ways. Those who used to shy away from hiring women because they might marry and leave or have children and leave are now realizing that it is common to combine home and work whether the employee is a woman or a man.

One aspect of this situation has not changed as much. When 500 women were interviewed last year, many of them indicated that they still felt caught between their home responsibilities and their jobs. Many noted that they worked 40 hours a week on their job and at least that at home. Superwoman is beginning to realize that that is a role she need not play—perfection isn't necessary on all fronts for men or women, but far too many still are working toward that goal.

Laws have been written to make it impossible for bias to be sanctioned in the workplace—at one time, the man's job was considered critical and the woman's supplemental.

What is even more important is the fact that many men and women believe that these shifts have done away with the differences and that all is equal in the workplace. IT IS NOT! Let's look at some of those differences.

- Men merge their personal and business goals; fewer women do.

- When men are tested on behavioral tests, many show the same behavioral style at home and at work. In contrast, a number of the women tested did not. They played different roles to meet different demands.

- When a child is ill, we are not at all surprised when the mother takes off, but many would be quite shocked if the father did so (some are beginning to assume that role now, though).

- The approach to personal strategies for success differ, too. Men ask, "What's in it for me?" and women tend to consider the process and design the plan.

- Professional women are now asking the same question, "What's in it for me?" and that's good!

- Teamwork is fostered during the formative years in part through the involvement in team sports—few schools field mixed-gender teams and most female teams get less attention and far less adulation.

Let's look at teamwork. When the well-known authors, Margaret Henning and Anne Jardim, did a survey, they secured some fascinating insight into the impact of such involvement. They asked what it was like, what had been learned, and what was needed to stay on the team.

WHAT DID YOU BEGIN TO LEARN?

It was boys only, teamwork, and hard work plus preparation, practice, practice, and more practice.

It gave you a sense of belonging, and if you were knocked down, you had to get up again.

A team needs a leader because motivation or the lack of it depends on the coach.

Some people are better than others but you had to have eleven.

WHAT DID THOSE WHO STAYED ON THE TEAM LEARN?

Competition, you had to win.

Cooperation to get a job done—you had to work with guys you wouldn't choose as friends.

Losing, what it felt like to lose.

You win some, you lose some.

How to take criticism...

> You don't get anywhere without planning and
> you have to have alternative plans.

> Once you know the rules, you can bend them
> and influence others.

Many of these personal rules will stand these "boys" in good stead in their adult careers—these same lessons are there for girls, too—if they play in the same games and on similar teams. It is interesting to note that the most prestigious sports for girls are NOT team sports, but individual sports—tennis, swimming, skating, golf, and gymnastics. Could this make a difference? Probably.

Before going any further with this comparison, let's have you do something. How do you see risk. Jot down your answer in the space below:

If you follow a typical pattern, you will have responded differently if you are a male than if you are a female. Women tend to define "risk" as something one avoids and something that impacts on the present. Many men respond in light of the future, and a number see it as a means of moving into a more positive future, at that.

Our styles also differ—more and more we are seeing that gender does not determine your style, but experiences may. It has been fascinating to administer an assessment instrument we developed to both men and women and see how differently they approach it. Many of the man note that it asks them to fill it out in light of what is expected on their job, they immediately say, "From my boss' point of view?" The majority of the women who have filled it out have not even asked, and when asked from whose point they will fill it out, many say, "Mine." success in the marketplace demands that we satisfy the person who brought us in, that we take the extra initiative and indicate a loyalty to the company and a dedication to the job. The 4:45 dash is not the best way to move up— even if there are children at home with a sitter. It is important to realize that success extracts a price, and the one willing to pay that price is the one who has the best chance of advancing. Of course, the old school tie still helps, but its power is declining.

Successful interaction is vital to personal growth and advancement. This means that we must learn to work effectively with others—even if we would prefer never to do so. Friendship in the workplace is often more important to women than it is to men if we are to believe many of the studies. Emotionalism has no place at work, and women have learned this. There is still enough concern that Diane Feinstein, former mayor of San Francisco, once said that the best advice she had to give women in business was "Die before you cry."

When asked what their greatest problems in business were, the 500 women in our survey noted the following:

- not being taken seriously.
- being given titles with no authority.
- chemistry
- not being included in meetings.
- trying to run a home and a career (job).

When men were asked the same question, they noted the following:

- limited opportunities for advancement.
- few openings at the top.
- the need for a degree which is often only a union card.
- little, or no opportunity to be creative.

Interesting differences, don't you think. Even so, there are commonalties that need to be considered. Those whishing to move up—no matter what the gender—need to SET GOALS, DESIGN A GAME PLAN, ASSUME RESPONSIBILITY, BE FLEXIBLE, BE CREATIVE, and BE WILLING TO GROW AND CHANGE AS NEEDED.

This means that each of us needs to couple the tools provided in this book with a strong SENSE OF DIRECTION. A recent university study indicated that only about 5 percent of us have set goals, and only 2 percent wrote them down to review consistently. If this is true of you, **change**. Take time to determine the route through life you will take and consider writing down at least five goals. If you have trouble thinking of any, consider these points:

- at least one should relate to your career plan with a specific timeline.
- another should relate to your personal growth and knowledge/skills base.
- one should deal with your business relationships.
- one should deal with your personal relationships.
- and another should relate to those areas that will enhance your self-esteem.

Then go on to take some very important POWER STEPS.

- learn to read and understand people.
- practice until this knowledge is part of you and is the basis for all of your interactions.
- take responsibility for your actions.
- learn to be assertive (not aggressive)
- go "the extra mile."
- develop a positive attitude and keep it by making certain that whatever you put in your mind the last 30 minutes of each day is positive, since you will replay it 15 times during the night.
- be flexible—remember how easily that which is brittle shatters.
- and be open to change.

The last point is one of the most important ones in this book. Those who can accept and adjust to change are those who are willing to step out of their comfort zones and grow, and only through growth can we move toward our full potential.

KEY POINT # 12

Successful interaction is vital to personal growth and advancement in the workplace.

APPENDIX

SUMMARY OF KEY POINTS

1. YOU ARE RESPONSIBLE FOR THE WAY YOU RESPOND TO PEOPLE.

2. OUR SUCCESS IS TIED CLOSELY TO OUR ABILITY TO RELATE TO AND INTERACT SUCCESSFULLY WITH OTHERS.

3. IT IS NOT WHAT YOU KNOW BUT WHAT YOU DO WITH WHAT YOU KNOW THAT PROVIDES THE RESULTS AND DETER-MINES THE WINNERS.

4. OUR VALUES GUIDE US, AND OUR ATTI-TUDES—WHATEVER THEY MAY BE—ARE AN OUTGROWTH OF OUR VALUES SYS-TEM.

5. WE ADJUST TO THE SITUATIONS AND PEOPLE WE ENCOUNTER IN ORDER TO IMPROVE RELATIONSHIPS AND OUR CHANCE OF INTERACTIVE SUCCESS.

6. PEOPLE SELL THEMSELVES ON IDEAS, PRODUCTS, SERVICES—SOME ARE MORE RESISTANT THAN OTHERS BECAUSE IT TAKES THEM LONGER TO SEE THE NEED AND RECOGNIZE THE "FIT".

7. MANY SUCCESSFUL INDIVIDUALS USE STRESS TO SHARPEN THEIR ENDURANCE AND COPING SKILLS INSTEAD OF LETTING IT BECOME A BURDEN AND AN ENEMY.

8. IF WE CAN FIND A WAY TO LINK OUR HIGHLY CREATIVE PROCESSES TO OUR GOALS AND ASPIRATIONS, WE WILL LITERALLY BE ABLE TO BRING ABOUT THE "IMPOSSIBLE."

9. POWER IS NO LONGER CONSIDERED A "RIGHT," BUT SOMETHING THAT IS ACCEPTED ONLY IF IT IS NEEDED FOR DEVELOPMENT OF THE ORGANIZATION OR THE SUCCESS OF THE TASK.

10. THE CHOICE OF STAFF, ITS PLACEMENT, AND THE PROMOTIONAL POLICIES ARE THE KEY FACTORS IN THE SUCCESS OF AN ORGANIZATION.

11. DECISIONS MADE BY TEAMS ARE BETTER UNDERSTOOD AND ACCEPTED BY THOSE WHO MUST IMPLEMENT THEM.

12. SUCCESSFUL INTERACTION IS VITAL TO PERSONAL GROWTH AND ADVANCEMENT IN THE WORKPLACE.

SELF CHECK

Circle the appropriate answer.   Copyright 1987

1. I PREFER:
   a. corporate attire and an "old money" look.
   b. to be stylish and well-dressed.
   c. conservative clothes and business suits.
   d. to be neat and subdued in my dress.
   e. casual clothes regardless of the occasion.
   f. to not have to worry about fashion or style.

2. I TEND TO:
   a. speak rapidly and speed up when excited.
   b. use illustrations, images and gestures when I speak.
   c. speak in a controlled and measured manner.
   d. be precise and careful in my word selection.
   e. be assertive and unconcerned about details.
   f. be shy, polite and control my emotions.

3. I TEND TO:
   a. be in control, assertive and—at times—aggressive.
   b. be warm, friendly and sociable.
   c. be relaxed, congenial and conservative.
   d. be open-minded, well-organized and tentative.
   e. be independent, challenging and erratic.
   f. be quiet, reserved and unemotional.

4. IF I HAD THE PERFECT SETTING (choose home or office,) IT WOULD:
   a. be decorated in muted colors and expensive antiques.

b. be filled with color, plants and pictures of living things.
c. conservative and non-formal.
d. have a good layout or flow, be traditional and well-maintained.
e. be unusual and different.
f. be functional, practical and with limited decorations.

5. IF I COULD CHOSE THE PERFECT CAREER, I WOULD:
a. be in a leadership position.
b. be in a job that permitted me to interact with people.
c. be in a field that permitted me to use my specialization
d. choose one that required precision work and attention to detail.
e. be an entrepreneur.
f. select a career that permitted me to use my logic and analytical abilities.

SCORING: Count the letters. If the majority of the letters are "a", then you are a LEADER. If "b" predominates, you are a PERSUADER, and if "c" is the letter which appears most often, you are a PATIENT PERSON. Those who have more "d's" are CAREFUL PEOPLE, and those with more "e's" are INDEPENDENT. The RESERVED PEOPLE will find that they have more "f" scores.

It is important to realize that you may well be a combination of styles and alternate their use. In most cases, people are a combination of two and sometimes even three.

PEOPLE CHECK

Don't guess about what a person wants or doesn't want, likes or doesn't like, responds to negatively or positively, fill this out, and KNOW. Even if you have just met, or haven't yet met, but know something about them, you can do a quick study that will give you the insight needed to ensure effective interaction, communication, and results.

1. DRESS IS AN IMPORTANT CLUE TO BEHAVIOR. DOES THE PERSON WHOM YOU ARE INTERESTED IN KNOWING MORE ABOUT APPEAR TO BE:

a. dressed in the corporate tradition—old money look,

b. stylish, well-dressed, and dressed to attract attention,

c. conservative, close to—but not quite—stylish, understated, fashionable—but perhaps not this year's fashion,

d. neat, subdued, and in matching apparel,

e. casual, non-compliant—but quietly so,

f. unconcerned about appearance, possibly coordinated, but not stylish?

Note appropriate letter _____

2. PEOPLE'S SPEECH PATTERNS AND TEMPO ARE EXCELLENT INDICATIONS OF STYLE, PACE, AND DRVIE. DOES THE PERSON IN WHOM YOU ARE INTERESTED APPEAR TO BE:

a. one who speaks rapidly and speeds up as he/she goes on,

b. one who uses images, is persuasive, wordy, and emotional,
c. one whose speech is controlled, measured, slow, and lacking in animation,
d. precise and careful about word selection,
e. argumentative, and unconcerned about details,
f. shy, polite and unemotional?

Note appropriate letter _____

3. WHO WE ARE IS USUALLY REFLECTED IN OUR MANNER AND MANNERISMS. CIRCLE THE LETTER THAT MOST APPROPRIATELY DESCRIBES THE MANNER OF THE PERSON IN WHOM YOU ARE INTERESTED.

a. authoritative, "know-it-all," in control, assertive, and possible aggressive,
b. friendly, sociable, impulsive, and enthusiastic,
c. relaxed, genial, conservative, and controlled,
d. open-minded, dependent, insecure, and well-organized,
e. erratic, independent, and challenging,
f. quiet, reserved, blunt, and unemotional.

Note appropriate letter _____

4. WE GENERALLY SELECT, OR DESIGN, OUR SETTING IN A WAY THAT REFLECTS OUR PERSONALITY. ASSUMING THAT THE SETTING WAS SELF-DESIGNED OR SHAPED, WHICH OF THE FOLLOWING BEST DESCRIBES THE OFFICE OR HOME OF THE PERSON UNDER CONSIDERATION?

a. muted, expensive-looking, but in the old-money tradition,

b.   colorful, warm, with pictures or drawing of people or living creatures, plant-filled,

c.   conservative, non-formal, secure, traditional,

d.   good layout or flow, traditional, conforming, neat and tidy,

e.   unusual, different, no real attention given to appointments,

f.   Spartan, pictures of things (even blueprints), functional, gadgets on display or near-at-hand.

Note appropriate letter _____

5. IF GIVEN A CHOICE, WE USUALLY MAKE OUR CAREER SELECTIONS IN AREAS SUITED TO OUR TEMPERAMENTS, SO IF AN INDIVIDUAL IS COMFORTABLE, OR HAPPY, IN HIS/HER WORK, IT IS AN EXCELLENT CLUE TO PERSONALITY. IS THE PERSON IN WHOM YOU ARE INTERESTED

a.   in a leadership position, or comfortable with responsibility

b.   in a position that requires interaction with people (sales, counseling, promotion),

c.   in a field which required that there be specialization in depth (teaching, accounting, law),

d.   in a field which requires precise work, attention to detail, or being perfectionistic,

e.   in a position that permits him/her to set the boundaries, make his/her own rules, "run the show" in an entrepreneurial way,

f.   in a career that requires logic and analysis, but does not require extensive interaction with others?

Note appropriate letter _____

Add up the scores. If the majority of the responses are (a), the person with whom you are dealing is a LEADER. If the majority of the letters were (b), then you are involved with a PERSUADER; on the other hand, if most of the letters were (c), you are interacting with a PATIENT PERSON. A majority of (d) scores indicate that the person is a CAREFUL PERSON, while (e) scores would note one who is an INDEPENDENT PERSON. The last type is a RESERVED PERSON, and this would be the case if most of the answers were (f). If the scores split evenly between two letters, read the descriptions for both styles.

THE SOLUTION IS IN YOUR HANDS

Most problems can be solved if we approach them logically and with minimal emotion. All too often we let our feelings get in the way and block our abilities to deal rationally with situations or problems. We have worked out a system that works EVERYTIME, but it means that you have to work everytime, too. The PROBLEM SOLVING SYSTEM is a distillation of the best of our earlier PROBLEM SOLVING WHEEL, the Xerox solution system, and a process developed by a professor at Stanford University in California.

Let's try it. Select a problem you haven't solved, or a goal you haven't reached, follow the directions, and take charge.

STEP ONE: State your problem or goal.

PROBLEM OR GOAL: _____

STEP TWO: List 11 reasons (excuses) why you haven't reached that goal or solved that problem.

1.   7.

2.   8.

3.   9.

4.   10.

5.   11.

6.

STEP THREE: Go back and cross out those in the above list that are "fluff" (or poor reasons).

STEP FOUR: Look at the items that remain and find a common element or elements that tie them together. Put those down. Now you are ready to move into the problem solving circle.

SOLUTION CIRCLE

STATE THE PROBLEM OR GOAL

LIST THE CAUSES NOTED

DETERMINE WHO WILL
FOLLOW-UP AND WHEN

BRAINSTORM SOLUTIONS

DETERMINE WHO WILL
IMPLEMENT IT AND WHEN

SELECT THE BEST SOLUTION

DESIGN A GAME PLAN

APPENDIX

AN INVITATION FROM THE AUTHORS

We would love to hear from you. Let us know how this works, or if you have questions, let us hear those, too.

Our staff and nine associates cover every aspect of human resource management. So, if you are planning a meeting or convention and need speakers who can motivate your staff to greater productivity or can design and custom-tailor a training program for you, please call us at (213) 822-3751.

> Elizabeth I. Kearney
> Michale J. Bandley
> KEARNEY/BANDLEY ENTERPRISES
> 563 Washington Street
> Marina de Rey, Ca. 90291

Kearney/Bandley Professional Series

Customers Run Your Company: They Pay The Bills

This book targets the needs of the 90's by giving you the strategies that attract, keep, and win back customers.

$12.95

Everyone Is A Customer

With this book you can build communication and motivational bridges. Read it and then duplicate the winning strategies.

$12.95

People Power: Reading People For Results

Use this guide to take the guesswork out of communication and interaction. "Read" people and **know** what they want.

$12.95

MLM Is Big Business: Fact Not Fiction

This book unlocks the secrets and shares the strategies of direct sales "giants."

$12.95

SEND IMMEDIATELY

563 Washington Street, Marina del Rey, CA 90291 (213) 822-3751

Name: _____ Title: _____ Date: _____

Company: _____ Phone: _____

Address: _____

City _____ State _____ ZIP _____

#	Item	Price
___	Customers Run Your Business (book)	$12.95
___	Everyone Is a Customer (book)	$12.95
___	Real Estate Match (book)	$12.95
___	Audio Synopsis of Everyone Is a Customer	$9.95
___	People Power (book)	$12.95
___	Solid Gold Customer Relations (hardback)	$16.95
___	The Hidden Side of Customer Relations (tapes)	$59.95
___	How to Increase Your Real Estate Sales (tapes)	$59.95
___	Quality Starts With Management (video)	$39.95
___	Reading the Jury For Results (video)	$89.95
___	Brain Check (IBM compatible disk)	$59.95
___	Prospect Check (IBM compatible disk)	$59.95
___	People Check (IBM compatible disk)	$59.95

Sub Total _____

Add $2.50 per book for postage _____

CA residents add 7% sales tax _____

Total _____

Total enclosed: _____

Check enclosed $ _____

Bill: ☐   VISA ☐   MC ☐

Card # _____

Expiration Date: _____

Signature: _____

Purchase Order # _____

° Call for special rates on large orders!

SEND INFORMATION ON:

☐ PresentationTopics
☐ Consulting Services
☐ Hiring/Training Tools
☐ Training Services

211